Someone Has Led This Child to Believe

Also by Regina Louise
Somebody's Someone

Someone Has Led This Child to Believe

A Memoir

Regina Louise

BOLDEN

AN AGATE IMPRINT

CHICAGO

Printed in the United States of America

Illustration on page 38: subidubi/Shutterstock.com
Photo on page 97: Reeed/Shutterstock.com

Library of Congress Cataloging-in-Publication Data

Names: Louise, Regina, author.
Title: Someone has led this child to believe : a memoir / Regina Louise.
Description: Chicago : Bolden, [2018]
Identifiers: LCCN 2018017046 (print) | LCCN 2018019321 (ebook) | ISBN
  9781572848153 (e-book) | ISBN 1572848154 (e-book) | ISBN 9781572842229
  (pbk.)
Subjects: LCSH: Louise, Regina. | Foster children--United States--Biography.
  | Abused children--United States--Biography.
Classification: LCC HV881 (ebook) | LCC HV881 .L64 2018 (print) | DDC
  362.73/3092 [B] --dc23
LC record available at https://lccn.loc.gov/2018017046

First printing: July 2018

10 9 8 7 6 5 4 3 2 1   18 19 20 21 22

Bolden Books is an imprint of Agate Publishing. Agate books are available in bulk at discount prices. For more information, visit agatepublishing.com.

For my sister, Cynthie, and her son, Timothy, and his sister, Sherry, and the innocence we all unwittingly lost.

For my mother, M.A.W., I've never stopped thinking about you, but I had to stop wanting you.

For my two brothers, wherever you may be.

Book One

Prologue

Throughout my journey, I have met thousands of children and youth who're biding their childhoods away in out-of-home care, and foster care, wondering what will become of them and wanting to know how to traverse the course they're on. From group homes to fictive kin homes, from transitional housing programs to emancipated young people with no place to land, these children are doing what they can to just get through another day. Some seem to thrive more than others, while there have been many who've felt they can't afford to dream beyond an inch of their breath.

This *is* the task of anyone who carries the burden of his or her own "unworthiness": to learn to give one's own self merciful favor while standing in the blistering heat of a primal wound; to seek refuge within one's own heart; and to wipe someone else's fatalistic narrative of what their life *will be* from their conscious, hand it back to the disbeliever, and say: "I believe this belongs to you."

A minute to collect myself

Even now, I am sometimes impervious to the jab meant to silence, demean, or deny the connection I seek. I give too much, too quickly, turn the other cheek, habitually terrified I'll be rejected, once again, marked for being *too big*, or *too mouthy*, or just more than anyone will ever want anything to do with, want to be around.

She's just too much.

I allow others to sidestep, push back, even obliterate my personal borders because I'm afraid that if I stand up for myself, if I defend against the limiting beliefs of who or what I "should be," given the gender, race, class, and unforeseen circumstances I was born into, then somehow, still, I will sabotage my efforts to fit in, to stay put, to belong to anyone willing to take a chance and associate with me.

She makes it so ain't nobody wants to see her coming.

In this *now* life, the one where I am sometimes a lover, an on-and-off-again friend, a voice for the unclaimed, a fictive sister to more folks than I can keep count, I tend to be overly concerned that these alliances, too, will cast me off and out. Sometimes I hear that I am "too therapized," and I imagine what is left unspoken is that my once being feral, and now rehabilitated, equals hypervigilance for the tiniest infractions. I have a high appreciation for keeping things just and evenhanded.

So, as if fueled by an unnatural impulse to gratify, I easily mete out *yes* when I mean to say *no*. I take up far too much space providing, allowing, and accepting, then backpedal the moment I sense I am vulnerable to rejection.

4

I charge trauma as the cause of these actions, the triumphant instigator that has no clemency for the destruction it detonates. Some traumas have the effect of deregulating the body's natural defense mechanisms. Sometimes I:

+ Freeze when I should fight;
+ Run when I should freeze;
+ Stay when I should take flight.

Trauma and its co-conspirators—shock, denial, shame, anxiety, anger, hopelessness, the inability to cope with daily life, and (the granddaddy of them all) post-traumatic stress disorder (PTSD) join forces to prevent our God-given personalities to come into their own. Much is required to stay stuck, frozen in a state of brokenness that demands a certain tending to, a sacrificing that gives nothing back but more of the same emptiness and inability to live this one life to its fullest. It begs for our complete devastation, trauma does, at times, and in many cases, takes nothing less. This is how abandonment lives in me.

"It's in relationships where we get wounded, Gina, and it is in relationships where we get healed," my therapist, Lainey, told me back in 1998 while I sat in her cozy San Francisco corner office. The J Church streetcar clanged its bell at half past six, switching tracks, changing lanes, consistently signaling my time was nearly up. I wore anxiety the way a monk wears a robe. Devotedly.

I'd shelled out $120 for fifty minutes of talk therapy; I frantically chewed up our time together hoping to save, retrieve, or gather up what was left of my raggedy sense of self. Nearly two decades past emancipation from foster care, I was *still* confounded by the weight I carried, the baggage of feeling unwanted, unavailable—to myself. My emotional malaise had a choke hold on the little bit of hope I was suddenly dying to hold on to. Although, at that time, I had no idea what constituted a *self*, something inside of me consistently rerouted my desire for self-destruction. *No, not this time,* a voice would say, *hang on, because God never gives you more than you can handle.* I wished I could've paid God to trade places with me.

Back in that room—where I now imagine the décor was designed to promote a stable sense of interior experience—everything from dolls as diversified as the United Nations, to animated figurines, sand trays, and Lainey's easy chair were all situated neatly, alongside perfectly shelved books to guide her quest to untangle dysfunctional worldviews. The well-worn sofa held me like I wished my daddy would have, the cushions worn threadbare, all velvety and warm. I burrowed down and in, my feet planted firmly on the ground in front of me. My hands rested on my thighs palm-side up, and only the Lord knew that I'd come begging for a blessing that day, something to make it feel like mine was a life worth living. Saving.

My life had reached a junction. Sure, I was a successful hairstylist by then, and loved the time I had with my clients, the trust they gave over to me, the human connection we shared, but even so, in my personal life I walked around in circles as though I'd witnessed too many wars. Ground zero. I was a shell-shocked soldier; I sometimes couldn't sleep, eat, or find meaning in the everydayness of every day. Grief and loss held me hostage in a game of whack-a-mole: no sooner did I confront one memory than another appeared, memories for which I had no language, all demanding resolutions for themselves. I didn't know that I was estranged from my *true* self. The janked-up part is that when you don't know *what* you don't know, the not-knowing becomes the means by which you let your mouth write checks your ass can't cash—like telling a white-lady therapist things that black folks weren't accustomed to saying. And before you know it, you've said far too much, there's no turning back.

My son, on the verge of puberty at that time, brought me much pleasure, and I guessed that the same protective factors that had driven me to take the managing of my own life into my own hands as a child—an optimistic attitude, belief in the power of hope and possibility, and cre-ative problem-solving skills—were also helping me to understand, now, that it wasn't my child's job to save me. That was my work to do: to find more resources, people, and coping mechanisms to reclaim my life from the horrors of my earlier experiences.

Lainey, eyes locked on mine, mirrored my breathing, my body move-ments, my affect; she aligned with me, blended with my bouts of dissoci-ation, all while simultaneously holding space and allowing one loss after another, like Lazarus, to arise and make their way toward the light.

The therapy, meant to be self-directed, often allowed pieces of the past to surface; some memories were startlingly clear, others not so much. Lainey asked me about one of my early caretakers and as I contemplated the question, I found myself sitting on the front porch of the house I grew up in, an asphalt-sided, tin-roofed shack. Roosters in the side yard cock-a-doodle-doo'd, and there I sat. Waiting with my belongings: a slip as nightgown, a change of panties, and a pair of mixed-to-match barrettes in a Safeway brown paper bag. Peach cobbler cooled on a side rail, chili beans simmered on the stove behind me. Home. And the want for my mama, Ruby, caught—like an insufferable jawbreaker—halfway between my throat and the back of my tongue. The taste of orangesicle; the pain of a scuffed knee, skin curled around the wound and was soft like pattern paper, caked with blood and gravel. The memories caught me by surprise. Snatched me back.

"Gina, tell me what you remember about your mother," Lainey asked within a month of our initial meeting. Panic stood where my mother should have been. I searched for a clear picture of her face, crossbreed features, her feet or hands, the texture of her hair. Her smell. Nothing. The longer I rummaged inside myself for familiarity with the woman I hardly had the chance to know, the more aware I became that my own mother wasn't mine.

Lainey never pushed. She only asked powerful questions meant to probe and gently shift my understanding of the relationships I had or didn't have. Then she'd step back to allow room for whatever presented itself.

Sometimes Big Mama, my first caretaker, showed up, not wearing her dentures, gumming my name as if she were right there beside me. "Ghee-na," she'd whisper. The taste of her fried catfish and coleslaw made my mouth water. Eventually, Ruby visited me by way of a whiff of her Pall Malls, or the sound of her full-bodied laugh. I was rarely, if ever, able to discuss both my mother and father in the same conversation. But every so often I'd get a glimpse of a tuft of hair that hung like dried pussywillow from a broad nose, and associated that half-remembering with my father, Tom, and just as quickly, I'd retreat into disgust at how the stiff hairs moved up and down when he spoke to me.

Finally, I consented to trying Eye Movement Desensitization and Reprocessing (EMDR), especially when Big Mama came around. I used it to process many of my memories, but for some reason, Big Mama, and my inability to articulate what she meant to me, brought out a grief that could knock me into a spell of speechlessness. The fact that I was learning that I was somebody worthy enough to belong to someone in a once-upon-a-time kind of way proved mind-boggling in itself. "Find a memory of Big Mama, Gina," Lainey would instruct, "Follow it until a feeling emerges." Once I had the memory, or feeling, we'd identify the specificity of what was happening. And the moment Big Mama got off that Greyhound bus and left me in Georgetown to travel to wherever I was headed, alone with no explanation, my stomach muscles contracted, my legs drew up toward my chest, my eyes watered, nose tingled, and although my mouth opened wide, no sound came out. I was preverbal. Lainey moved in closer during these times, a hand on my knee. "Look at me," she'd urge quietly, at first. "Look at my fingers, Gina," her voice louder, an overtone away from a direct order. "That's it, keep looking at me." Once she had me, she'd put two fingers at eye level and move them back and forth like windshield wipers. "Back and forth, Gina," she'd say, "just keep following my fingers." Back and forth and I'd follow her movements, back and forth, back and forth until the pixelated sense of the unspeakable gave way to a space where I could breathe more easily, sit in the tenderness of the moment, and allow for language to come back on its own terms. Eventually, the feeling of sadness or overwhelmingness softened into me. It was as if I had more room inside myself, my heart. Although depleted, I'd feel better able to think about my past in ways that allowed me to remember without terror and hopelessness. I became better able to face and transform the shame, to turn my devastation into my motivation.

Unlike "all the king's horses, and all the king's men," over time I learned how to stay with those recollections, how to recognize and defuse those triggers one little step at a time. To calm my nerves, I tried whatever modality was available to me at the time: acupuncture, massage, special tinctures to calm my nerves, cranial sacral release, yoga, hypnotherapy, self-compassion techniques. From each I took what was offered and used it as mortar to patch my life back together again, reordered it so that I might better locate myself in time. Space.

Time and time again, though, I found myself marooned in my own awareness that while I'd done all the right things—grew myself up, accepted that my rejections were not personal, made it a practice to follow the Golden Rule—I *still* had to learn there were no guarantees I'd ever get what I really wanted: A good enough mother. Relations who indulged my need to be their daughter, sister, cousin, granddaughter, aunt, or partner. Someone willing to stay.

I've learned that who I am today is a direct result of the ordeals I have endured: rejection, loss, abandonment; being born a bastard. None of these facts were ever intended for me, or directed at me as though they were ever deliberate, or personal. I've come to understand that my mother's abandonment was a tributary that flowed out of her mother's leaving, which flowed out of her mother's mother's disappearing, and all the streams lead back to the river of these women's refutations: being born black, blisteringly poor, and invisible. The trauma of belonging to trauma is congenital.

Taxonomy

As a child, in 1972, I lived in a sharecropper's shack on land that was handed down from generations of black bodies toiling away beneath the roiling Texas sun, picking cotton and blueberries, and shovel-whipping rattlesnakes the size of a three-ply Manila tug-of-war rope. I learned that to stand up for myself—in relationships—was to risk being a whistle-blower, troublesome, spiked good with the Devil's blood. I was dangerous. I was to be rid of.

Say another word and I'll beat the black off you right where you stand.

These were Lula Mae's words. She was the eldest foster child of Newt Cavanaugh and his wife, Rosetta, also known as Big Mama, my mother's keeper, and eventually mine, too. Lula's threats, booming with detestation and spitefulness, spewed from her mouth on a daily basis. She made it clear how *f—d up* it was that our mother had abandoned my sister, Cynthia, and me to be taken care of by folks who didn't want to be *bothered with the burden in the first place*. I was ten years old and believed in Jiminy Cricket and that if I made a wish upon a star, the wish would come true. I also believed Lula's threats of terrorization. We all did.

I wished like hell I didn't live there.

I'd witnessed firsthand how the adults in my world did business, how their intimidations were never idle, and how satisfied they were to extract recompense from the rear end of anyone who'd committed an unexpected offense. Expectations were hidden, like land mines; we didn't know where they were until they exploded in our faces. *Your behind is mine now*, is how Lula Mae usually put it. As if it wasn't humiliating enough to get it wrong. As if that fact alone, that we'd shamed ourselves, wasn't payment enough.

On several occasions, I watched as Cynthia failed to protest the accusations that she was a lying, conniving, don't-nobody-want-you kind of child. That she was bad for thinking she deserved more than our caregivers were willing to give her. That even though she was Big Mama's favorite, and could do no wrong, when it came to Lula Mae Bledsoe, favoritism gave way to a hard row to hoe. My sister became a target of Lula's own backwoods ideologies about a child's fate should the rod be spared.

I listened as my soft-spoken sister took her time—to buy time—to slip the elastic waistband of her culottes down the length of her coffee-colored legs, the fabric etching ashy marks into her dry skin. She'd strip down to her nakedness only to be wet down with a water hose and whipped: for stashing away a soiled sanitary napkin, a salad dressing sandwich, a matching pair of lace trimmed socks, or anything she wanted to keep secret beneath the mattress of the bed I shared with her.

I was the one who gently dropped the Mercurochrome onto her raw flesh, careful not to let the tip of the dabber touch the open wound, staining the pink spots a shade of red that after a few days faded to brown. I hoped against hope my mother, Ruby, was at any second going to show up and do the same to Lula. My sister was the one who'd introduced me to Mercurochrome; there were many times she'd had to use it on me.

I had a front row seat to the violence and terror that played out right in front of my childhood eyes. Fistfights over money, women, and the men who had plenty of both but refused to shell out a cent for the children they had sired out of wedlock. This left a trail of bastards a mile long for anyone who gave a good goddamn to come along and collect us for the promise of a few dollars here, a block of government-issued cheese there. Love was never an interchangeable commodity.

I was either eight or nine years old the day I saw the story in the city newspaper. I came across a notice about a shooting that had occurred the previous night, somewhere near South Sixth Street, in a motel whose name I've long since forgotten. The notice stated that when police officers arrived on the scene, one Ruby Carmichael, a black female of South Austin, had been shot in the lower abdomen by the girlfriend of an unidentified male. The victim had survived surgery and was in critical condition, and expected to survive.

What I knew at the time: my mother's name was Ruby Carmichael; it was folklore that she had a penchant for other people's property; she'd learned to want no one, or no thing, that wasn't trifling or incapable of feeding her need for the extreme repetition of her own nightmares washed back with a fifth of scotch or any other malted whiskey or any other woman's boyfriend. Or husband. The gun-toting girlfriend had accused my mother of stealing her man. My mother, in return, chastised the woman for being unqualified to hold on to her own man, and refused to take the blame for something the girlfriend brought onto herself. The woman shot my mother at point-blank range. Unlike my sister, my mother invented ways to stand up for what she believed. Right or wrong.

I loved our mother for the legendary proportions her behaviors took on, her fiery ways of getting what she wanted, but I had no use for her not having that same fire to want us.

Although that was not the first self-inflicted wound my mother had experienced, it was the one that would catapult me even deeper into a childhood chock-full of adverse experiences. Nothing would ever feel safe again.

The day Lula Mae attempted to beat the black off me started out as an ordinary day. I awoke with the expectation of attending the carnival that had taken up residence in the Safeway parking lot four blocks from where I lived. Some of my classmates were going to be there as well, and we hoped to meet up at the cakewalk. My intention was to win a cake and share it with my friends. I was cranked up.

Lula called me into the house from the curb I'd been standing on while rocking her teething daughter, Ella. The baby seemed to prefer the sound of motor vehicles passing over asphalt to anything else, and since it kept her quiet so that Lula could stay tuned to her new favorite show, *The Young and the Restless*, I had given the child what she wanted: a half hour or so of rocking on my hip while we watched car after car pass by. Then I'd handed Ella off to Dorothy Jean—who'd told Lula that I had been standing in the middle of the street playing dodge-the-car with Ella.

Lula wasn't one to miss out on an opportunity to point out a wrongdoing in the hopes of feeding on the pitifulness of the accused, nor an occasion to "take it outta your ass." This time, the cut-off water hose whistled through the air as she laid into my body with a force I'd never known before. Fury burned across her face in waves of fine ridges, and then thick folds of skin, until her mouth became a sinkhole of rage.

Lula blew fire. She claimed that since I was one-part devil and the other part my mother, it was her duty to beat the desires of both out of me along with the blackness of my skin. I understood, then, that to be black was bad, to be black was just cause to be obliterated, to be black was a blasphemy that not even God could protect against. I was on my own.

Nevertheless. I wasn't my sister. I wasn't some "still waters run deep" kind of girl too afraid to tell anyone how I felt about the way they treated me, too afraid to be my own savior. I heard, nearly every day, how much of a "bull in a china cabinet" I was, and how I needed to be more like my sister, quiet to the point of being self-erased. No thank you. I had made a pact with God: should Lula beat me again, it would be a sign from him that I should leave. I did not belong to her. I belonged to one day in the future when I'd get to be who I wanted to be.

So, like I imagined my mother would have done had she faced Lula down, after blow upon blow of her battering my flesh, I turned on Lula and caught the water hose in midair. My hand stung. It didn't matter.

"I didn't do nothing wrong," I screamed at Lula. For a moment, we stood arms raised above our heads holding on with all our strength to that cut-off green water hose.

"I know you didn't just grab that hose," Lula Mae screamed as Big Mama plowed through the door. "You gonna be a nothing." Big Mama wedged herself between me and Lula.

Make good on the pact you made with God. Keep your word. She hit you again, it's your sign, the one from him (God). Time to go. She tried to kill you. Leave. Now. Run. You can do this. Run. Don't look back. Run. Don't stop till you know you'll be safe. Run.

"Just like your no-count mama, a nothing!"

Over the juniper shrubs, through the wall of cypress trees that shielded the front of 2524 South Fifth Street, I ran. I sped down the footpath that led past the 7-Eleven at the corner where my street, the only place I'd ever known as *home*, crossed West Oltorf.

"You gonna be . . ." Lula Mae's words hissed at the backs of my heels.

I circled back over Oak Crest Street, hightailed it through the parking lot of San Jose Catholic Church where, on many an Ash Wednesday, I'd stood and watched through the windows as the priests, in their voluminous robes, made the sign of the cross with their large white hands on the center of people's foreheads, using what I imagined were cigarette ashes. Oh, how I envied them and coveted the protection of their God. I ran, my flesh wounds burning in the heat of that late August night, alongside Juanita Avenue until I reached South First Street, near my elementary school, Molly Dawson, and I didn't stop until I collapsed on the front lawn of Sonya Perez's house. Sonya was my best friend.

My favorite Bible verse helped me when nothing else could.

For God so loved the world that, He gave His only begotten Son and, that Whosoever believeth in Him should not perish, but have everlasting life.
—John 3:16

Repeat until you can breathe again, until you forget the throbbing, the sting, the pain, until you no longer want to beat the black off Lula Mae one thundering blow after another.

. . . a nothing.

My mother, Ruby, paid a high price to belong to something, someone, as well as nothing or no one in the end. My sister revealed this story to me six decades after the fact: in 1946, my mother was found sitting on the floor in the middle of the kitchen in the house she lived in with her mother, her sister, and the ghosts of her two dead brothers. Her mother lay there, four days dead. Minnie was my first and real grandmother's name. My mother was three years old. Her sister, Toni, five years older, held on tight to their mother's slack hand. As the legend has it, my grandmother drank a bottle of potassium hydroxide because rheumatic fever had taken her two sons from her. The neighbor and family friend who happened upon the situation, Rosetta Cavanaugh, took in my mother and her sister.

While staying at the Cavanaugh compound, Rosetta reached out to one of my mother's uncles and informed him of what had happened, and shortly thereafter this man, Alphonse, a veteran, started coming on the regular to visit Minnie's girls.

I wasn't privy to how the everydayness of time passed for my mother while at the Cavanaughs' because her life wasn't archived like that, it wasn't captured in red-letter moments that added up to days worthy of remembering, then of being tied up with baker's twine into sweet bouquets to be passed on to her daughters in an heirloom trunk. The story that did make its way to me—by way of my sister—was that my own mother's uncle took quickly to her beauty, as many men had, with her copper-penny-red hair, skin the color of a sun-kissed Georgia peach, her pillow-soft lips. It was rumored that my mother owed her good hair to her mother's mother, who was part Apache, and to her father being half

Mexican. My mother loved to bathe, and evidently her uncle Alphonse loved bathing her. His hand-to-soap, hand-to-cloth, hand-to-skin water ritual led to the unfathomable, and at thirteen my mother gave birth to her first child, my sister, her second cousin. Uncle Alphonse fucked us all out of belonging.

By what metric can these generational sufferings be measured?

When my mother gave birth to Cynthia, she passed on to her the gifts of a photographic memory and the ability, at ten, to draw Tippy from the back of a Richie Rich comic book, which warranted a visit from an Art Instruction School representative. Our mother failed to attach to my sister. Our mother prided herself on wearing a size two before having us kids. I say that when my sister arrived into the world bare naked and innocent, she gave shape to our young mother's incomprehensible shame. I say, our mother didn't know that the secret in loving my sister, her first child, could become the foothold to loving herself.

Cynthia became Rosetta Cavanaugh's girl.

During the short and intermittent moments I spent with her, my mother was highly unpredictable. Without signal or sound, her moods slid from her in bites and fits and scratches. She kicked, she brandished a .44 Magnum pistol (always pointed at my sister), and she threw firebricks at the hood of her male friend's brand-new car. She slammed doors so hard the shuddering stuck to the skin like napalm; the burn of it followed me around for years. She threatened, "I brought your motherfucking ass into this world, and I'll take your black ass out!" I imagined she could do just that, take me out. Who was there to give a damn if she had? I imagined it was a power that all black mothers had—a fundamental right to course correct for the misery of bringing a bastard child into a world that was indifferent to whether mother or daughter lived or died. Her threats were classic.

When she wasn't working eleven at night to seven in the morning at Seton Memorial Hospital with the elderly, or in some private residence "cleaning old-ass white people's asses," she was bedridden from migraines, too many cigarettes, and way too much scotch. She was barely able to stand the sight of her own self, let alone the desperation of my wanting her attention, her approval, a small acknowledgment. That desperation must've leaked from me, my wanting her backed up in the space between us like liquid in a clogged IV cord. To this day, I'm not sure I'd recognize my mother if she were to pass me on the street. Trauma, not unlike my mother, is sometimes an innocent, self-serving narcissist; both are incapable of knowing their true worth, both are incapable of giving the smallest of mercies.

I've never known the exact date, or the conditions, under which my mother determined it was a good idea to leave me and my sister with people who let a grown man—Uncle Alphonse—indulge himself on the innocence of her adolescent girlhood, only to then sneak away in the night. Now I tell myself that my young mother did the best she could with what she had, and at the time her best probably dictated that we would be better off, my sister and I, with the devils she knew as opposed to the ones she didn't.

Today, I am better able to understand how we were all haphazardly stitched together, back then, by the harrowing consequences of what we didn't know.

Book Two

My father was almost famous

Tom Brock's album, *I Love You More and More*, was released in the summer of 1974. It was expected to soar to the top of the R&B charts. The great Gene Page, who'd worked with the Four Tops, Barbra Streisand, and Marvin Gaye, arranged many of the songs on Brock's début LP. The album had four songs on the A side and four more on the B side, and the Love Unlimited Orchestra backed up the vocals. I can't imagine what it must've felt like to have 150 musicians show up just for me. Tom Brock had it good. I suppose.

There he sat, my father, on the cover of this album, on a beige settee with embroidery stitching. He was wearing a red velvet tuxedo jacket with black lapels over a white turtleneck. Pimping. An oversized ficus tree loomed in the background. He held a glass of red wine in one hand, although I never remember him having a drink, while the other hand touched the arm of a dark-skinned woman. She was not my mother. Their eyes, like the lighting in the room, were lowered, smoldering. Locked. I haggled with an aggressive seller on eBay for nearly a week to get a copy of the CD. In the end, I paid $75 to hear my father's voice again. Smooth.

He wrote hit songs for Glodean James, Gloria Scott, and for the Sultan of Soul himself, Mr. Barry White. Barry produced Tom's album. He played the piano, my father, faster than Jerry Lee Lewis, and taught himself classical guitar. His lead song, "There Is Nothing in This World That Can Stop Me from Loving You," débuted on the pop charts at number ninety. Yet his album was a dud. It would be another thirty years before that same song would have its day, courtesy of Jay-Z, who sampled it into his blockbuster hit "Girls, Girls, Girls." The $30-here, $50-there royalty checks I get from BMI—*now*—are the most I've ever received from my father.

He lived in Los Angeles back then, Tom did. The Westside. He also kept residence in Richmond, California. And in 1975, when I was twelve, I lived with him in a bungalow in Richmond, with his Norwegian wife, Nadine, and their three children. By then he'd lost everything that mattered to him: his record deal, his relationship with Barry. His relationship to spatial reality.

Nadine's children, two girls and a boy, had their own bedrooms in that little house on Downer Avenue. I slept on the couch in the living room. The couch's arms were frayed.

I lasted nearly two months.

My father was a "high yellow" black boy. Eighteen. My mother was seventeen. Tom met Ruby at the high school she'd later drop out of in order to take care of my sister, who by then was five years old. I first met Tom when I was nine or ten—the exact age I cannot say, because a million things happened all at once back then. Ruby had sent me from Jacksonville, North Carolina, to stay with my father because her live-in boyfriend, Mr. Benny, asked me to let him touch my nipples. He said he wanted to do to me what the "middle finger" stood for. He chewed toothpicks, twirled them around his tongue in between his requests.

One night, after I had been in Richmond a month and a half, I wanted to hear my mama's voice. I missed how she called me Gina-girl. "Gina-girl," she'd say, and I'd stop whatever it was I was doing; the sound of her calling me by her favorite name for me, like hungry fingers, grabbed hold of my heart and pulled me to her, quickly. The fact that she'd taken a moment from thinking about herself to think about me was like digging for gold and finding it in my own backyard. The moment of the finding was all mine, forever. No one could take that moment from me. At that time, I lived mostly with Big Mama, with only brief and random trials of living with Ruby to see if we could "dig" with another, you know, like jibe with one another. I made every word, look, touch, and way she called my name stick for as long as it could. I had to talk to her.

But Nadine, whose toes resembled mini television sets the way the wide nails smashed into the meat of her feet, controlled all access to communication in the house, including the kitchen phone. I could not stand to be near her, or those feet. She said I didn't have permission to call my mother, given I had no money to pay a phone bill.

Should I call my mother?

I took one of the kids' Magic 8 Balls and shook it, and shook it, and shook it to determine whether or not I should call my mother.

I wanted, I wished, I dug

I snuck into the bedroom of my father and his wife, which was off-limits. There, atop one of the matching bedside tables, sat a pink princess telephone. I'd never seen anything like that phone in my life.

Tucked between the nightstand and the side of the bed, I slowly lifted the receiver. My fingertips fit perfectly into the grayish, indented squares. The *boop boop boop* of the keypad excited me. The phone rang twice. I was seconds away from hearing my mama.

"Hi, Ruby. It's me—"

"Get off my phone!" Nadine hollered from the kitchen of that thin-walled house that felt no larger than a child's playpen.

"Hey now, Gin—" my mama said just before the line clicked dead.

I slammed the receiver down.

"You cain't do that!" I yelled repeatedly from my spot on the floor, then into the kitchen and inches from Nadine's face. She had a way of staying silent, her obsidian-colored eyes staring at me fearlessly. She was a school principal. My desire for my mother kept me forever in detention. For a short while, I curled up like a prawn on that scratchy-to-the-touch sofa, and pleaded with God to send my mother to me.

I wanted to swim in the White Shoulders perfume she slathered on.

I wanted her to never stop calling me "Gina-girl. Gina-girl. Gina-girl."

I wanted the odor of Pall Malls on her breath mixed with watered-down scotch to waft over me just once more before whichever one of us died.

That night, I walked straight on out the front door and marched what felt like thirty city blocks to the big laundromat on Rheem Avenue. Whenever my friends and I ditched school—Downer Elementary, which was right around the corner—we'd go to the laundromat and race up and down the aisles in the laundry baskets.

I waited for the last woman to pull her clothes from the dryer, and when everyone had left, just before closing, I laid the upper half of my body inside that dryer to stay warm. I stared at the black-and-white speckled enamel dryer drum as though it were the night sky. I looked for the Big and Little Dippers, hoping to wish upon them that my father would snap off on Nadine for my leaving. He'd make her sit down and write:

I'm sorry, Regina.
I'm sorry, Regina.
I'm sorry, Regina.

A thousand times, until she meant it.

I wished that at any moment my father would come looking for me, and once he found me, I'd agree to go home with him. I wished that I could let him touch me, carefully, and in so doing, I wouldn't break, or be ruined, or even get accused of being a "prick tease," like Ruby had said about me after Mr. Benny. Prick tease, she called me, "you a nasty little prick tease." I had no idea what such a thing meant. Anyway, at the time I knew better than to let what she said hurt my feelings because I had to save the hurt for when it really mattered, like when she broke her promises to come and get me, to take me home with her. Anyway. It wouldn't have much mattered: I wasn't afraid to stand up to anyone, except Ruby. I knew she'd have no reservations about cursing me out, or reaching beneath her bed to pull out her gun, and point it at me.

If he came, my father, I promised myself to let him take my hand, and hold it, if only long enough to lead me to the car, buckle me in, and tell me it was natural to want my mother, even if she didn't want me. I'd want him to sit with me in the unwanting and show me how to need myself, show me that even if she didn't, he did.

I dug donut holes out of the garbage can of the bakery next door. Sitting on the bench out front, I dusted off any trace of mold or dirt and popped the sweet balls into my mouth. Every now and again, I imagined my father's metallic-green Lincoln Continental with the suicide doors driving by, and just as he would catch sight of me, park, and then kill the engine and head toward me, I'd make him disappear. *Psyche.* I'd go back to eating the donut holes.

The next morning, I crawled from behind the bakery's garbage cans, where I'd slept through the night. Hungry, I headed to school. I loved school. Even though I had difficulty paying attention, controlling my impulses, and watching what came out of my mouth. I preferred reading ahead, or solving a math problem without showing how I worked it out, or yelling the answer out loud. Something in me urged me to do so, especially when my teachers called on other children again and again and they'd gotten the answers wrong, or stuttered at a speed deserving of my long and equally drawn-out eye-rolls. I was a smart-ass child. I did not have patience for favoritism not coming my way.

At lunchtime, in the cafeteria, I became the Six Million Dollar Man and I cut in the food line. A boy my height poked me from behind. He asked me to move.

"Make me," I said. Another boy standing in front of me also turned around; he was the twin of the boy behind me. Despite their talking smack and their weak attempts to push me back out of the line, I managed to get a tray, plate of food, milk, butter knife, and fork.

I held my head high as I handed the cashier my yellow free-lunch ticket and headed to a table in the middle of the cafeteria. Out of nowhere, one of the twins pushed me. I recovered my footing in just enough time to turn and slam the tray into his face.

I fought them both.

Then I ran. I became Lindsay Wagner. I was the Bionic Woman. There was no one I could not defeat.

An hour or so later, I arrived at my friend Mary Cosentiniano's house. She always left her bedroom window open, just in case I ever got in a pickle and needed a place. I hadn't gone the night before because I wasn't going to wear out my welcome. I knew better, my resources were limited. Also, I knew that my stay would be limited, and I'd promised myself to use her room only if I had no other choice.

It was good, her house with its mother and father, two sisters, and an older brother who banged the life out of his drum set in the garage. He let Mary sing back-up on "Rhiannon," while I did my best rendition of a smoky, throaty Stevie Nicks. I sang hard to drown them both out and he drummed along pretending he was Mick Fleetwood. Jimmy was going to be somebody, bar none. Me too. I was going to have a solo career like Karen Carpenter.

Hanging out with the Cosentinianos was better than wasting time trying to stay out of the way at Tom and Nadine's, with their three kids and not nearly enough room for "his bastard." Not to mention that by this time, Tom had begun to hallucinate. He imagined the government had unleashed wild animals in the neighborhood. Sometimes he disappeared for days, coming back when he felt like it. He'd bring meat and hang it to line dry in the kitchen, proclaiming the world was on the brink of the end days, and that he needed to prepare for prophesized apocalypse. He also said that Nadine was the cause of their youngest son's inability to breathe. He locked Nadine in the closet, where she stayed. I wonder if he'd ever heard of asthma.

At Mary's they all sat around a table at the same hour each night. The father would come home from collecting garbage, toss his gloves in the garage, kiss his wife, and say hello to whomever he came upon next. The mother, her bushy hair always flat on one side from her daily naps, brought plates of food and set them between a vase of dandelions and a

Tupperware salt and pepper set. I loved the gold *P* and *S* on the slender-waist bottles and swore to myself that one day I, too, would buy a set when I threw my first Tupperware party.

They'd all eat as if the Italian wedding salad and gnocchi smothered in red-meat gravy was the best meal they'd ever eaten. The way they talked between bites, and laughed with mouths full of food and hands whirling and flapping this way and that, made the hush among my own kin deafening.

Shortly after that phone episode, my father received a call from a woman claiming she'd recently given birth to his son. Tom moved back to Los Angeles.

I had nowhere else to go.

Garbage bag caught on the windowsill

Two months after my father left in 1976, I paid a visit to the woman in whose charge he'd left me. By then the money he'd promised to pay her for my keep had stopped and the phone number he'd left was no longer in service. It quickly became a hit or miss whether I could sleep at Ms. Rosecrans's.

"You in there, Ms. Rosecrans?" I knocked on the back door of an unkempt house. I wore Ditto's Jeans, a white T-shirt with a red glitter rose, and raggedy red Converse sneakers.

"Ms. Rosecrans? Ms. Rosecrans if you in there I just come for my stuff!" No answer.

I peeked through the kitchen windows. All clear. I dragged a garbage can over to the window, stood on it, and pushed my way inside the kitchen. I moved fast. One after the other I searched through kitchen drawers until I found a Glad garbage bag. I'd lived long enough with strangers to know, in my bones, the things they didn't say but would want to beat me half to death for if I didn't somehow, magically, already know.

I was safe if I stuck to:

1. Never using the Lord's name in vain, i.e., saying: Goddamnit. Lord have mercy. For God's sake. Lord knows.
2. Never asking for anything other than what was given.
3. Never even *thinking* about discussing my own heartbreak.
4. Never. Ever. Getting so comfortable as to think I have a right "to anything in this here house."

I headed for the stairs. Then suddenly, all 200-plus pounds of Ms. Rose-crans came raging around the corner toward me. My sixth-grade best friend's mother, the woman my father had agreed to pay for keeping me, placed herself between me and both the front and the back doors. There was no way out.

"Little good-for-nothing! Ain't nothing up in here belonging to you. Give me my bag back, now!"

Ms. Rosecrans snatched me by my hair. I needed that bag. I held on. We fought and she smashed my face into the corner of a wall. The two of us fell to the floor. Ms. Rosecrans tried to pull my clothes from my body: my pants, my T-shirt. I kicked at Ms. Rosecrans. Ms. Rosecrans grabbed hold of my left foot and attempted to remove my shoe.

"These is my shoes Ms. Rosecrans! They mine! My father gave me the money for them." The more I thrashed, the more I kicked, the tighter Ms. Rosecrans held on. I clawed and scrambled to hold the base of the banister while doing whatever I could to get free.

"Your so-called daddy ain't paid for a goddamned thang up in here, freeloader! You not even worth the price of these-here shoes."

Kicking free, I ran up the stairs and locked myself inside the small bedroom with its two twin beds, six-drawer dresser, and closet full of everything and anything Anica could think to ask for. Anica, Ms. Rose-crans's daughter, was my friend, once upon a time. They were "doing the good Lord's work" by giving me a bed, even though my "no-count" father had reneged on his payment agreements. Using a chair, I barricaded the door. Ms. Rosecrans came up the stairs. I crammed what I could into the ripped garbage bag and the back of my pants pockets: a mood ring, a cigarette, a plastic baggie holding the tissue that held the last kiss my mother had given me.

Ms. Rosecrans pummeled the door, the sound juddering through me. The pounding became increasingly frantic. "I'm a kill you," Ms. Rosecrans screamed. I picked up a phone receiver and dialed the operator. "Lord knows you nothing but a ingrate!"

"Operator! Can you connect me to the police department?" I whispered, watching the door.

Boom!

The door gave way. Ms. Rosecrans rushed into the room toward me. I disappeared out the window, jumping two stories, and leaving the garbage bag caught on the windowsill.

Until the sun towed daylight into the sky

Sunday morning, May 2, 1976, was my thirteenth birthday. I awoke in a two-window room in Martinez, California. The windows were chicken-wired shut and reinforced with nuts and bolts. The Edgar Children's Shelter was an orphanage. By orphanage I don't mean a Dickensian poorhouse like in *Oliver Twist*. This wasn't the *Annie* version either. Edgar Children's Shelter was a county-maintained receiving center that accepted displaced children from all over the San Francisco Bay Area on a twenty-four-hour basis.

It was a one-story ranch-style dwelling on an acre of scorched earth. The county had kept painting and repainting the clapboard building a yellowish beige till it took on the color of pale phlegm. Even though Edgar was a place to deposit unwanted children, the county had done its best to blend it into the surrounding middle-class neighborhood by adding an eight-foot cyclone fence with cedar slats around the property. These slats shielded Edgar from the outside world, as did bushes that smelled like cat piss. A worn American flag waved from an equally tired flagpole.

I had arrived in the middle of the night. Two police officers led me from the back seat of a squad car to the intake room, where Mr. Potter, a bald-headed man who looked as if he'd just swallowed the moon, processed my arrival. Sweat dripped down his forehead and temples, and his belly pressed hard against his shirt, his elastic waistband, and his desk.

"Do you have any next of kin?" he asked.

I shook my head no.

"Do you know your father's whereabouts?"

I shook my head no.

"What about your mother?"

What about my mother? I'd wanted to ask Mr. Potter. What is it, exactly, you want to know about her? Had I the gumption, the pluck, or the sass that I normally carried around with me like a bag full of buckshot, I would've pounded Mr. Potter with what I knew about my mother. I would've told him:

> *After Big Mama sent me to Jacksonville, North Carolina, to live with my mother, my mother then sent me from Jacksonville to live with my father in Los Angeles, California; then my father sent me back from Los Angeles to Jacksonville to live with my mother, her two sons, and her live-in boyfriend, Mr. Benny; after that, my mother moved her two sons, Mr. Benny, and me to Augusta, Georgia; and finally, my mother sent me to live with my father in Richmond, California. My father left me in Richmond with my sixth-grade best friend and went back to Los Angeles. As a result of his disappearance, I turned myself over to the police. The police, as you can see, brought me here.*

When Mr. Potter had completed the intake procedures, he pushed a white button and spoke into a wall speaker. Within moments I walked down a long, sterile, overly bright hallway behind a small woman the color of an uncooked pinto bean. Bright orange panic doors opened and closed with the click of the metal air handle underneath a flickering exit sign. My red Converse, the ones I'd stolen on a dare from K-Mart, screeched across the sterile linoleum floors. A heavy-duty ring of keys jangled like sleigh bells from my escort's waistband every time she moved. I told myself anything would be better than the laundromat, or the streets. Ms. Rosecrans.

Shortly thereafter, Gail Maddy, the woman who'd led me to the girls' section, sat across a desk from me in the staff room. White concrete walls, beige file cabinets, and grey indoor-outdoor carpet. A foot-long, black tactical flashlight lay on the desk next to a clipboard and a red leather-bound book titled *Daily Record*. Miss Maddy explained that I'd arrived during the graveyard shift. My mother had worked those same shifts, and just hearing the words made me more at ease.

"I see here that Mr. Potter asked you about your mother," she said looking straight into my eyes. "Is there anything you wish to tell me about her?" I turned my head quickly and stared through extra-thick safety glass into the shadows of a darkened room just beyond where we sat. Ms. Maddy explained that she'd be the one to stay in our section through the night. She'd keep watch over us until the sun towed daylight into the sky. Then, she'd hand over the giant key ring to the a.m. relief staff and exchange details concerning the girls whose names were handwritten in the red book. Morning rounds would begin.

Love has its own smell

"Good morning, Pumpkin," said a perky white woman, whose root-beer-colored hair moved about her shoulders in ropey whorls, the key ring now jangling from her wrist. I sat up in the rickety bed. She had my attention. In between the spaces she moved, from bed to floor, floor to bed, shaking this one's toes, picking up discarded blankets and restoring them neatly at the foot of that one's bed, shaking another one's toes.

"My name ain't no Punkin'," I said, rolling my eyes and swiveling my neck, two moves all little black girls I knew had: our way of establishing ground, letting whoever it was know we weren't to be trifled with.

"I know," the white woman said, and placed her hands upon the tops of my knees. I cringed. Big Mama had long ago warned me that white people were the only folks she'd known who could "go barefooted with hot pants on in the dead of winter without catching they death in sickness." She'd told me to stay clear of them, unless, of course, I wanted "their ways to rub off onto me." This woman smiled generously. She spoke to me in a way I hadn't been on the receiving end of before. Though the new situation was unnerving, as I didn't know what I'd gotten myself into, I felt the tightness loosen in my gut.

"Your name is Regina. Welcome to the shelter."

"What's your name?" I asked.

Cream of Wheat, warmed PET Milk, vanilla with a bit of brown sugar—that's what the smell brought to my mind when Miss Kerr crouched down to meet my gaze. Her breath reached across the world that lay between the two of us. Closed us in. The scent fixed itself upon me and clung to my skin, staining me the way a baby bird is stained when a human hand touches it. Like the bird, I was marked forever. Love had its own smell.

"Please, come with me." I scooted off the bed and followed her lead. We bypassed the staff room I'd sat in the night before and walked against a crowd of kids—no older than I was—who seemed anxious to get outdoors. They slammed through the panic doors and assaulted the air with swear words and arm farts, and their angry feet stomped down hard on the cracked, brittle earth. The scraggly ways they were dressed, ill-fitted corduroy pants, unironed shirts, the jitteriness in their eyes, all mixed with the smell left in their wake. It reeked of unwantedness.

In another room, called the nurses' station, Miss Kerr studied a series of Xs on an outline drawing of a human body. The whole thing felt like we were on one of those television detective shows.

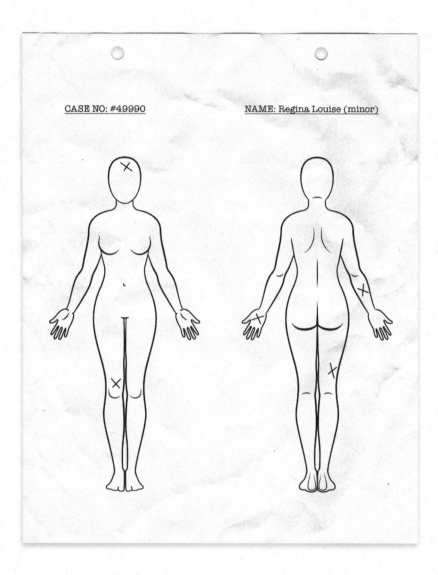

Miss Kerr turned the form toward me and pointed to the X on my forehead.

"Who did this to you?"

I sat quietly.

Miss Kerr waited patiently.

Ms. Rosecrans got away scot-free.

After Miss Kerr and I finished in the nurses' station, I grabbed my personal belongings from the bedroom. In the staff room, I handed over:

a) my clothes,

b) a half-smoked Kool cigarette,

c) a mood ring, and

d) the baggie with the tissue, in exchange for a pair of shorts and a shirt.

Ten ways to best use toilet paper

- ☐ Blow your nose in it
- ☐ Wrap it around your hand until the wad is thick enough to use as a menstruation napkin
- ☐ Stuff it into your bra to prevent you from looking like a tomboy
- ☐ Make shoes fit that are too big for you
- ☐ Tear it, then twist it into pieces, and use as a roller
- ☐ Pretend you have the Kentucky Fried Chicken man's moustache
- ☐ Spit nasty food into it: Peas. Okra. Cod Liver Oil. Ambrosia Fruit Cake. Flush it
- ☐ Hock a loogie into it
- ☐ Wipe your behind
- ☐ Wipe snuff-juice from around Big Mama's lips
- ☐ Dry your face before you really get something to cry for
- ☒ Hold the last kiss your mother ever gave you

Make a wish

Swensen's Ice Cream Parlor was filled with high-pitched voices, kids running freely and wildly through the room. And no one seemed bothered by the racket of it all. The adults did not slap the kids upside the head because of how rotten they were; there was no chastising about how they were going to burn in hell for being so damned troublesome.

Instead of bemoaning the fact that a party was happening at all, families clustered around tables inside red leather booths that resembled half-eaten sour cherry balls, and music poured from the tabletop jukeboxes. Electricity filled the air, which somehow matched how I felt inside—the feeling that I was at May Day festivities, back at Molly Dawson Elementary, blossomed in the center of my being.

I had been the first one to run beneath the parachute during the May Day dance, as the belly of the thing billowed above my head, and there I stood for one glorious moment inhaling it all and allowing the thrill of being alive to sink into my pores. For that moment, anyway, I had an idea of what it meant to simply be a child, had the pleasure of being plain old me.

As I recompose memory into meaning, those scenes are a reminder to me of what being happy looked, sounded, and felt like at my old friend Mary's house. The truth is that those strangers at the ice cream shop, and my friend Mary's family, had made loving a child for all of who she was look so easy to do.

Helium-filled balloons bumped against Swensen's ceiling, their colorful ribbons trailing along, and I wanted to grab them one by one. I wanted to grab them all and run nonstop through California, Arizona, and the top of New Mexico until I reached South Austin, until I reached 2524 South Fifth Street, where I'd find Lula Mae sitting there, in front of her black-and-white television with the aluminum-foil rabbit ears and the vise-grip pliers used to change the channels. I'd interrupt her prime-time drama and shove those balloons into her face and say, "See, I'm halfway on my way to being the somebody I always knew I was." Then I'd set those balloons free.

Miss Kerr walked toward a table in the middle of the room. The workers wore white short-sleeved shirts with red stripes, and bow ties, khakis, and silly hats that reminded me of Bert from *Mary Poppins*. Three guys sang happy birthday to a little boy. He swung his head from side to side, and flicked his tongue out at the folks gathered around him. They laughed, pointed, and snapped a Polaroid. He was not accused of being ungrateful. Or stupid. It's as if they expected him to act the way he did, and he was happy to oblige them. The folks I came from never seemed to have the patience to tolerate happiness, especially mine. Perhaps an act of kindness brought with it the expectation of my wanting more of the same. Perhaps it was better to pretend I had no needs than to face the reality that even if I did, no one was particularly interested in meeting those needs. That may've been one of the first times I witnessed—up close—the differences between how whites and blacks treated their children. Poverty has a way of dissing possibility, shaming it back to a sense of futility, a sense of uselessness.

This was an incredibly impressionable time for me. And without knowing the socio-racial implications of what it meant to be displaced, black, and female, all I wanted was to be *needed*, to be celebrated, and to be accepted for the gutsy girl I saw myself as.

Before I ever had a chance to protest, a gaggle of workers made their way through the parlor, toward our table, carrying a white cake sprinkled with every color in the rainbow. The cake, in all its splendor, stopped in front of our table. The boy holding the cake set it down, and it read *Happy Birthday, Regina* in pink icing, and all I could allow myself to do was laugh. I was speechless. Embarrassed. I had no experience for this.

Another someone offered me balloons, and yet another blew into a kazoo to establish pitch. Then they sang *me* happy birthday, and without realizing it, I'd moved closer to Miss Kerr. "Close your eyes and make a wish," Miss Kerr directed. I closed them, and Miss Kerr placed her arm around me and scooched me even closer.

I don't ever remember feeling so safe, so okay with being touched before that moment.

It was amplifying, her kind of joy. She made a wish fulfilled look and feel as though that was the way life was supposed to be. And in those moments, it wasn't about my being black or Miss Kerr being white. In those moments, it was more about the freedom from the oppressive weight of failed dreams.

I sank into her embrace, and somewhere in the holding on, I made a wish to never have to let her go.

Not so unlike falling in love with a boy, or a boy with a girl (except for a kiss), I fell in love with Jeanne Kerr shortly after that trip to the ice cream parlor; shortly after we got back to the shelter those kids who got to go home on the weekends to be with their own families—Tammy, Jordy, Trudy, and Dana—argued to stay behind and hang with the "nice white lady." They wanted some of what she was giving me; they wanted to be seen and heard and called names that lifted their lives up from the lowest common denominators of scarcity, loss, and being unwanted to the unlocked secrets that lay inside oneself when love begets love; they wanted to feel what it was like to have their lives spinning around, and moving up and down, like they were their very own carousel rides. I was destined to be a swan. The choice was mine.

I was happy to have Miss Kerr all to myself. It made facing the facts about my situation bearable. No one from my bloodline or otherwise came to visit, called, or wrote me love letters about how they missed me so much and just couldn't wait to set eyes upon me once again. They put no hands around my slender shoulders, and pulled me close with the intention of never letting me go, showing me there was nothing I could do to not belong to them. It was as if they only existed in my mind and there was no tangible evidence I ever happened to them. There were no photos of me with Big Mama, or with my sister, Cynthia Ann. There was no one to pick up a sentence where I'd left off and finish telling my story, our story of what it meant to belong to one another. Inside though, I missed like hell sitting between Big Mama's warm thighs on a Saturday morning, the smell of yeast biscuits rising beneath a cheesecloth towel above the kitchen stove. The feel of cool Texas dirt beneath my bare feet was one I'd never soon forget, the way it felt like walking on baby powder, silky. Soothing. I missed far too many things to admit to myself that I was slowly losing the only family I had learned to love, back then. Given the enormity of the loss, and the fear of the grief, it was far easier to reject them and make them wrong for not being able to love or want me.

Weekend leftovers

My father, Tom, lived only a thirty-minute drive from Martinez and ECS, but he somehow managed to concoct a world of his own where I did not exist, a world that allowed him to keep his paternity in question. Still. I called him, wrote letters to him, and sent messages via my social worker, Alma Martin. I never wanted him to feel the way I felt: invisible.

I once spent an entire day crocheting what I'd hoped would become a beanie for my father to wear on his head, but somehow, I miscounted the required stitches, and the resultant accessory was more likely to be worn on a "weenie." Although it was considered highly inappropriate, I'd made an effort I was proud of. I wrapped the multicolored coverlet, tied a bow around it, and sent it to Tom via Ms. Martin, whose eyebrows arched high into her hairline, like two tattooed clothes hangers, when I'd shown her my gift. In all honesty, I never once tried to understand how weird as hell it was to give my own father such a thing. The Christmas before, he'd given me a jar of pickled pigs' feet. I'd thought he was attempting to be funny, something he rarely was. He was serious, though. And the way I saw it: he'd started the gifting of weirdness disguised as regular, therefore he would appreciate my comeback.

I never knew what Tom's responsibility was to me, as my father. It's as if he came from out of nowhere, got a good look at me, changed his mind, and crawled back into a place where he didn't want to be found. I never saw Tom through the eyes of a *real* daughter because I didn't know what that was. When I looked at him I saw stranger, I saw "beware." I sometimes think he preferred it that way: minimize the expectation to mitigate the disappointments. Nevertheless, I was willing to try and give him a chance to get to know me. And although I stood there like a circus clown, marshalling his attentions toward me, he didn't see me. I felt like I "was" the no there there.

Also, growing up in an institution had its limits. It felt as if my very existence held a pejorative meaning. As a matter of fact, looking back, it happens that all my behaviors, as well as those of the children I lived with, were placed on a continuum of being either all good, or possessing varying shades of pathology. The middle ground belonged to an elite group that established the behavioral norms against which all else was measured; a group we'd all been ousted from for one reason or another; and that group was our own families.

Tom never personally responded to the gift, or to the birthday card, or to the pecan pie Miss Kerr had helped me bake for him. I was so proud of that pie, all the pecans I'd shelled by hand. I heard from Ms. M that he thought I needed help—that our relationship had run its course and more desperately than ever, I needed the Lord.

Instead of pining over my parents' rejection of me, I fell deeper in love with the way Miss Kerr called me "sweetheart" when we weren't at the shelter, when we were driving down the street on our way to an outing, maybe swimming at the YMCA in Pleasant Hill or on a 7-Eleven run. The way she said it, "sweetheart," made my heart feel as if I were a sun with a thousand rays reaching out to touch every part of life—like anything I thought to do was possible simply because I'd been called a sweetheart. I'd learn over time how to conjure up those feelings in order to connect with the absence of her, along with the goodness in me.

I was head over heels when—because of my running away one day to get to her house before her shift at ECS ended—I was allowed to sleep over at Miss Kerr's. It was close to 9:00 p.m. when I sneaked from my bed, shoes in hand. I tiptoed past the staff room and headed for the side door next to the bathroom. I quietly pushed on the panic door handle and once outside, I ran while sliding into my Converse, then jumped the fence that surrounded the facility.

Earlier that day, Miss Kerr had taken a few of us girls, the "weekend leftovers," on a drive. Along the way we stopped by her apartment at 140 Flora Avenue. I made it a point to imprint her address onto my brain by repeating it six times. By the time I set out to find my way back to her house, I acted as if I was on my way home.

"What are you doing here?" Miss Kerr asked, as surprised to see me there as I was for her to ask me why I was there. When she'd brought me over, it was cool; in my mind, my inviting myself felt just as cool. Miss Kerr invited me in *and* called the overnight staff at ECS to explain the situation, and that she'd bring me back the next day.

She presented me with my very own toothbrush, and squeezed toothpaste onto it. It was not so unlike what Big Mama would've done from time to time. I took my time to brush: I wanted that moment to last. Miss Kerr handed me a long white nightgown that buttoned from the collar to an inch or so above my ankles. Louisa May Alcott, or one of the girls from *The Waltons*, had nothing on me.

Anything

"You can be anything you want, sweetheart," Miss Kerr told me one day while helping me pack my belongings into yet another Glad garbage bag. Miss Kerr was a dream-shaping apostle who proselytized the importance of making one's dreams come true; her words baptized me into the river of believing. I *could* be whatever I wanted to.

I wanted to be . . .

1. Famous
2. A ballet dancer
3. A singer
4. A beautician
5. A model
6. A counselor like Miss Kerr
7. A mother to ten children
8. A social worker to help kids like me
9. Different from my mother
10. Different from my father

300 vs. 602

"Are you a 300, or a 6-oh-2?" the mayonnaise-colored girl with the pinky-length pigtails had asked, swirling her neck as if to energize her question. Her name was Jordana. She had a pinched nose that preferred to head north while the rest of her small face stayed put. Her outer lips, always lined in black Maybelline Expert Eyes eyebrow pencil to appear larger than life, were mere brackets for the slabs of Vaseline that greased the flesh of her mouth. She was *Fly*. The hair that circled her face was held down with the same Vaseline in rattail-combed s-curves and flattened-out curlicues. She set the trend way before Michael Jackson. She was cool like that.

"I don't know," I told her.

"Whatyoumeanyoudon'tknow?" she shot back while her chagrin for my stupidity sprung up all over her face.

"Ain't that what I just said?" I fired back, wondering why, all a sudden, this girl wanted to talk to me. Other than Miss Kerr, I hadn't made many friends at the shelter. Kids came and went quicker than I could learn to pronounce their names.

"Ain't that about a B?" she said, "I know you ain't try to get smart with me, roadkill?"

"My name ain't roadkill," I said.

"It may not be now, but if you keep on getting smart it will be." Thinking she was being funny, I laughed. Hard. While it took her a minute to catch on that I wasn't going to go where she may've been trying to take me, she eventually chimed in and laughed. She thought I was funny. I could have fought her if that's what she wanted, but I knew better. More than anything I wanted to increase my chances of getting to spend as much time with Miss Kerr as I could, and a fight would set me way back.

We slapped each other five and turned a play to establish territory into a bond of burgeoning affection.

From that moment on, Jordana became my first, and only true, friend at ECS. She was a street kid from North Richmond who was forever truant and flat out refused to step foot onto the school's grounds, let alone walk into a classroom. She peddled uppers for her brother on the side but was busted for ditching school when she sold to an undercover truant officer. I, too, shirked off school now and again, but for different reasons. When things were right in my life, there was no place I'd rather be than in school—the learning, the teachers, the reading, and writing, the madrigal choir, and art—and the only thing that kept me from it was my need to have a place to stay.

I let Jordy, as I came to call her, school me on the differences between a 300 and a 602.

Ways to become a 300

1. When you done had your ass whipped and taken from your family
2. Left behind in an abandoned building for days on end with no running water
3. Your mama takes off with a man promising to return soon as she can
4. Daddy goes to jail
5. When your blood won't take you in

Ways to become a 602

1. Threatening at the top of your lungs to bust the windows out of your boyfriend's car after you caught him with another girl, and someone hears you and calls the police
2. Pissing on the lawn of the one who reported you to the police for threatening your boyfriend
3. Following through on the threat and busting windows out of your boyfriend's car

I was a 300. A ward of the court. So was Jordy due in part to her age and the fact that her boyfriend refused to press charges and she got off with a warning, that time.

I got glad

By the time Ms. Martin's white county car, with the gold-emblazoned stickers of the State of California plastered on both the driver and passenger side doors, peeled out of the driveway of the random house where she'd dropped me off with the hopes of my belonging to some random family, in an equally random section of the East Bay, I'd already said my pleasantries to both the wife and the husband and had scoped out my escape route: the window of the bedroom I'd be expected to be grateful for, whether I liked it or not.

The room had one bunk bed and a twin. None of the sheets, quilts, or blankets matched: there were checkered fitted sheets, napped from one end to the next, the checks colliding with faded and flowered top sheets with the kind of pattern I'd only seen on the cover of a jigsaw-puzzle box. It was dazzling to the point of dizzying. The whole thing smacked of down-on-their-luck folks taking in kids for the money and even if they weren't, by then I'd had more than my share of that kind of *feeling* in a home. I knew enough to know it would take far too long to learn the difference, if they liked me for me, and by then I'd most likely have burned a bridge for one infraction or another, leading to termination of the placement. My motto became: reject them before they had a chance to reject me. Someone, I can't remember, accused me of having "rich girl dreams, lined with poor men's pockets" and implied that beggars can't be choosey. I never saw myself as a beggar. I made sure to leave before I wore out my welcome.

The house and its rooms and beds were nothing like Miss Kerr's house, with her soft sheet sets and the comforter filled with down that she'd called a "duvet." It sounded fancy, royal. *You can be anything you want, sweetheart.* I wanted to be wrapped in fancy. *You can be anything you want, sweetheart.* This house didn't match my dreams of what it felt like to be wanted.

I wanted to be back with Miss Kerr.

Black

"You are *black*, you know, Regina?" Gwen Forde blurted out, as if to remind herself that she'd cornered the market on what black was supposed to look like on a fifteen-year-old abandoned black girl.

Before I knew it, I'd "ran off" Ms. M. I'd heard it through the grapevine that Ms. M had but one more chance to place me in a permanent foster home before she'd be replaced by a new worker, one who could handle me. Time after time, Ms. M dropped me off at one placement after the other, as if hoping that any family would fit, maybe like a hobo to a free meal, or a hand to a glove, skin to flesh, perhaps even like a fish to water. My response was mostly the same: hells to the no. I had other plans, if anyone had bothered to ask me.

In walked Gwen Forde, the woman who was to become my social worker/nemesis for the duration of my status as a ward of the court. There we sat, Gwen Forde and me, on that first date, in a small visiting room adjacent to the office where intakes took place. Ms. Forde was a petite, coffee-colored woman who wore twinsets (the outer sweater always draped around her shoulders, a caped crusader in cashmere), A-line skirts, and kitten heels. Two strings of glossy pearls looped around her neck like Mamie Eisenhower. Gwen always acted brand-new, as if she had never met a child like me, one half wild, the other half unafraid to glom on to anyone I thought liked or loved me. A moisture-heavy mole sat perched above her upper lip, a soft licorice drop, and it moved when she spoke. Her mole was an undercover operative.

Gwen Forde's Afro capped her head military-regulation tight, and if

I hadn't seen her face-to-face, if I hadn't been right there in the room with her, if I hadn't watched her tongue move rapidly around in her mouth about all the ways I was and wasn't being "black," with her practiced speech, each vowel articulated to its own sterile and syncopated rhythm, consonants cloaked in codified enunciation—had I not seen her, and only heard her voice, I would have bet my life that Gwen Forde was a white woman, maybe even Mamie Eisenhower herself.

A superior judge from the juvenile court division had appointed Gwen Forde to my case. Gwen Forde's job was to make sure that I got what I needed: somewhere to live; a decent family that would take me in as their own; and, to Gwen's preference, a family that was black. They must be "black," Gwen Forde contended, as though I were her opponent on the matter.

"The family will most likely be black, like you," she continued. "You do know, Regina, that you *are* black?" was both the systematic indictment, and accusation disguised as a question that lay beyond my childish abilities to understand. Each time I looked in the mirror, I saw a brown-skinned girl with a face full of freckles that I'd come to both love and defend. Because after all, supposedly everyone knew, black and white alike, that "real blacks ain't got no business having no freckles."

Was it not enough to be excommunicated from my family of origin, cast as an outsider? Perhaps, my being in foster care added insult to an injury that Gwen secretly nursed. Perhaps I was just one more reminder for her not to feel her own shame of what it meant to be rooted in an identity that was both invisible and startlingly inescapable. The fight was not mine, at that time.

Whenever Gwen Forde spoke to me, it became more and more difficult for me to listen to her speeches, difficult for me not to want to sock her in the mouth, to say, "Shut your damned mouth. Now, is that black enough for you?" Instead, I allowed my mind to take leave from wherever I was: the passenger side of the car, the courtroom, the lunchroom, the counselor's office, the visiting office, the stairs leading to the courthouse.

After the first sentence that began with "black," I was off and running. Searching. Dipping. Dodging. Confused. Whatever blackness she was trying to run on me, I wanted nothing to do with.

"Why do you always have to start with my being black?" I asked her once while eating a plate of spaghetti at the Velvet Turtle restaurant, her favorite. "What's the problem *you* have with the color of my skin?" I asked, my voice tight, impatience leaking through. Gwen explained that it wasn't about me, per se, so much as it was about the way I acted. "You act as if being black isn't good enough for you, Regina." As usual, I had no context for her statement. I began to feel as though I'd been struck repeatedly with a dumb stick.

Could she not see that I wasn't her equal, not a match for her? Having no actual reference point for what Gwen intimated only left us both that much more stranded from a common language that might've otherwise strengthened understanding between us.

Kids like me didn't have time to pay attention to adults' crazy ways of saying things. We were asked questions about our parents we had no answers for. The worst being: *What on earth did you do to make your family not want you?*

How do people pick themselves up—repeatedly—from the weight of such a question with the expectation of dusting themselves off, and keeping it moving, as though no offense was ever intended? That was some passive-aggressive shit. That's what kids like me had to learn to do.

I don't remember anyone who followed the Black Power movement, anyone who kept me and the other foster children abreast of what was happening on the front lines of black politics. I thought dashikis, Afro puffs, and fist-picks were fads, no different than Jordache jeans. To me, they were "tight" outfits that only the rich could afford, no matter if they were black or white. I wouldn't know about Martin Luther King, Shirley Chisholm, or Rosa Parks until three years later when I'd attend a public high school for the first time since grammar school, at seventeen and a half. Even if I wanted to take on the system, I would not have known where to get started. All the adults around me except Gwen were white: the counselors, the therapists, the judges, the teachers, and the volunteers. And as for the other residents, they seemed filled to the brim with wanting to know *whom* they now belonged to, *what* was going to happen to them, *when* they were going to find answers to these questions, and *how* they were going to make it through. I fought for what I could: my right to be loved. And as far as I understood it, love was the color of whoever was willing to love me back.

"You're manipulative, Regina. You've run from so many homes, I'm afraid there'll be nowhere else to place you." Anyhow: what did that have to do with my being black? I looked up the word *manipulate* in a dictionary. And not just *any* dictionary, but the one Miss Kerr had given me as encouragement to never move past a word I did not understand. If Gwen was so concerned that I went about getting my needs met by means that were skillfully intended to always be in my favor at the expense of another, what prevented her from showing/teaching me a different way? If vulnerability could be considered an antecedent approach to manipulation, and she were charged with mirroring to me my own sense of self-worth, who was manipulating whom? And what child is a match for such practices?

Flight risk

During the year and a half I spent intermittently at Edgar Children's Shelter, I failed more than twenty-seven trial runs to potential foster families in the San Francisco Bay Area. One county vehicle after another dropped me off in:

Pittsburg
Antioch
Stockton
Martinez
Sacramento
Richmond
San Francisco
Martinez
El Cerrito
Oakland
Martinez
Redding
Concord
Richmond
San Francisco
Pittsburg
Martinez
Antioch
Richmond

San Francisco

Martinez

San Francisco

Martinez

Stockton

Martinez

El Cerrito

North Richmond

Stockton

San Francisco.

Each time, I stepped out of the car carrying my personal belongings in either a Glad garbage bag or a brown paper sack. There was no room for shame.

When those twenty-seven placements "failed to take," sometimes it was because the men in those homes wanted to have their way with me—especially the home where the Preacher lived with his wife, son, and three daughters. Years later, while watching a television news program I learned that allegations of neglect and abuse were filed against this same family.

Gwen Forde was made aware of what was going on inside that house because I attempted, on every occasion I had, to tell her.

I went as far as to try and tell Gwen Forde—exactly—how the Preacher's son *really* was. I tried to tell her how the Preacher's son thought of himself as a "Pimp in the Pulpit." He prided himself on how he "hit it, and spit at it."

I told Gwen Forde how he peeped at me while I undressed through a small hole he'd drilled into the bathroom door. And how I stuck a Q-tip into the hole. He blamed the destruction of the property, the handmade hole, on me. An incident report was filed against me.

And then there was the time he walked by me, while I was getting my hair pressed by one of the other girls in the house, and leaned over and whispered into my ear how he'd rape me if I opened my big mouth about our little secrets.

Gwen Forde said that I was jealous that my hair was nappy, and not long and wavy and good, like the Preacher's daughters' hair.

I tried to tell Gwen Forde about how the Preacher's son waited until the household was asleep. How he'd open my bedroom door, slowly. How he'd spend what felt like hours tiptoeing toward my bed, then take his time to pull the sheet back. How the sound of his zipper drowned out my heartbeats.

How he led himself, bone in hand, between my sixteen-year-old thighs and tried to force himself into me.

How I pretended to be asleep, and fought him off at the same time thinking he'd think it was all a dream, and that I'd gone mad, and encourage him to make it end.

How his breath smelled of doo-doo and collard greens. How he threatened to "bust my butt-hole," just for fun, if I ever told.

How he said that I was the reason my mama and daddy hated me, wished they'd never had me, and looked forward to the day I died.

I told Gwen Forde what he said: "You ain't gone be the first piece of foster-girl poon-tang I'er had. You bastard girls, y'all's all the same. Don't nobody gives a damn about y'all."

I told Gwen Forde how he visited my bedroom off and on for the next six months. I told her that I wanted to leave.

She accused me of "making things up again."

She said that I was a natural-born "storyteller," with an "incredible" knack for exaggeration.

She said that there was no other place for me to go, that my reputation "preceded me."

She said that unlike the little white girls that came and went from ECS so quickly, I wasn't fortunate like them to have white daddies to write checks to finance their craziness.

She said that feeling bad about myself, my life, was a luxury I couldn't afford.

She said that what I needed was a black family, or at least "two strong black women," women who would see through my "cutesy girl" antics.

She said that white people were gullible and that's the only reason Miss Kerr liked me and that I had her wrapped around my finger.

She said that "truthfully" Miss Kerr felt sorry for me.

She said that I thought I was white.

She said that I was suffering from an identity crisis.

She said that I was "affected" and had no idea who I *really* was.

I asked Gwen if she'd want to take someone like me home with her given how black her own skin was. I asked Gwen, if I'm so bad, why would anybody want me, black or white?

I asked Gwen if it would be okay if I lived with Miss Kerr because she didn't seem to mind the way I was.

If disgust had held an audition for a much-needed spokesperson, Gwen would have been its poster child. Gwen threatened to place me in Napa State Hospital, in the children's psych ward, yet again.

Mostly, I ran from all those homes to be with Miss Kerr.

What do you see

December. 1977. The white county car skulked around the hills of El Cerrito, California, and I had become accustomed to calling the passenger seat "shotgun." Idling beside a curb, Gwen Forde spun the steering wheel until the wheels pointed toward the good doctor's front door. It was painted red.

Once inside, I took the seat offered to me by a woman I imagined was the good doctor's secretary, and while she was pretty, with her long Cindy Brady ponytail, she wasn't prettier than Miss Kerr.

The not-prettier-than-Miss Kerr secretary led me into another room. Behind a great big dark-wood desk wide as a door sat Dr. Cohen. His was a swivel chair. Behind him, on a long narrow table, were photos of what I imagined to be a younger version of himself with a woman, a boy, and two girls. The smaller girl held on to a ginger-red dog, an Irish Setter. "Daisy," Dr. Cohen said when I stared at the photo probably longer than I should have.

He stood, reached for my hand, and upon contact our hands wilted; I wasn't sure who was more afraid to touch whom. He got right to it, Dr. Cohen did. He picked up a large deck of cards and explained that all I needed to do was tell him what I saw in each card he held up.

It took a second for the affront to register. My skin tingled. I felt as if my entire existence were being challenged, as if the good doctor was trying to one-up me on the sly.

I sucked my teeth, and scoffed at the first photo. What nerve. Over and over I clenched my fists, repeatedly repositioned myself in the chair.

"Take your time," the doctor said, and I sat there, chewed my finger-nails, and rocked one leg up and down. This way, that way.

"Tell me," the good doctor said, "tell me, Regina, exactly what you believe you see in this picture I am holding up for you."

I saw a lot of images in the card he held up: a mean-looking cat, a pos-sessed pumpkin head, a pissed-off Wile E. Coyote, two bats French-kissing a large beetle bug. I saw how stupid it was for a grown man to pour what was obviously ink onto paper, fold it in half like a slow kindergartener, and then have no reservations to ask me what the hell it was. He thought me the idiot? If he didn't know, how was I supposed to know? He continued to hold one damned card up after the next until I gave him something he could hold on to, until I gave him reason to lift his fancy pen, and write something down onto that white notepad he'd scribble on in between hold-ing up those childish cards.

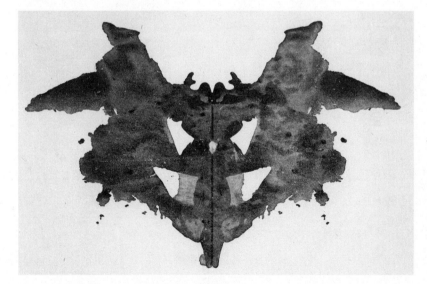

"I see two of them little bitty Mexican dogs fighting over a roasted marshmallow on a stick. No, wait," I said, "I see two of them little bitty Mexican dogs trying to hold on tight, with all of their might, to a pogo stick."

A couple of days prior to my appointment with Dr. Cohen, the staff at ECS had taken the girls' section on an all-day outing. In the evening, we'd been instructed to each collect a long stick in order to toast marshmallows over a fire. To my surprise, we'd made s'mores. They became my favorite. We'd also taken turns learning to bounce up and down on a pogo stick.

Day in court

It was June of 1978 and the day of my semi-annual dependency hearing, during which Gwen Forde and a judge would decide whether I was fit to live within a family setting, or should be placed in a Level 14 residential treatment facility.

The courtroom, small at first glance, seemed larger than Andy Griffith's. The walls, marbled black and white, were cold to the touch. I sat catty-cornered to the flagpole on the left of the judge's bench. My back was against the wall. My case was the only one on the docket that day.

"All rise," said a large man dressed in dark chinos and a matching shirt. The bailiff called out: "This is a dependency hearing for minor Regina Ollison, case #49990-16, born in Austin, Texas. Who represents the minor?"

Gwen Forde rose from her chair, raised her hand, and swore on the Bible to tell the truth, the whole truth, and nothing but the truth.

"Your Honor," Gwen proceeded, "for all intents and purposes, both of minor's parents have relinquished custody."

I sat quietly and waited. I hoped I'd get a turn to tell the truth, the whole truth, and nothing but the truth about what I wanted.

"Be brave, sweetheart," Miss Kerr had told me that morning. Miss Kerr had gone so far as to say that perhaps one day we could live together. She'd asked me how I felt about that. She'd read my mind, said what I couldn't. By then, I'd heard nary a sound from either one of my parents. I hardly ever thought of Big Mama, or my sister. But I was so glad Miss Kerr had the guts to ask me.

"You think Gwen would ever let that happen?" I asked, afraid that something bad might happen to me if I let myself believe I deserved the good she offered.

Miss Kerr promised to take me to Hawaii, to have us live among her relatives who lived there. She was descended from Hawaiian royalty and said they'd accept me as their own. She wanted me to feel comfortable in my skin, be around others who were my same color.

From that moment on, I secretly tried to piece together the scenes of what it would be like to live with Miss. Kerr. I saw myself in an "outside" school, where I'd get to raise my hand in hopes of being called in class because I'd studied hard the night before. I'd become the teacher's pet and get to leave class whenever I wanted. I'd become trustworthy. Miss Kerr not only watching, but cross-examining me until I got the right answer. I saw myself peeling the crumpled dollar bill and fifty cents that she'd give me for my lunch out of the front pocket of my jeans, and handing it to the lunch cashier. I'd dodge the shame that came along with a free-lunch ticket.

I'd learn to look forward to my birthday, and over time acquire a taste for my favorite cake, and not only have the courage to ask for it, but also, maybe, I'd learn to make friends again, like Trinity Rodriguez back in South Austin. Maybe I could even have my own party, in my own house, and invite my own friends. More than that, I saw myself, at the end of a long day, standing curbside, backpack heavy with homework, broken pencils, and crumbs from the cookies she would've sent with me, and picture-day forms requiring my parent's immediate attention. There I'd be, waiting for Miss Kerr to swerve around the corner in her blue Oldsmobile. She'd named it the Blue Swan. And just when I thought she'd perhaps changed her mind, and had decided to leave me there, because how could someone like her want me, she'd pull up. I'd get in. Off we would go, just like that, the two of us.

"Will minor please approach the bench?"

$4+9=13+9=22+9+0$ *is 31 . . . * $4+9=13+9=22+9+0$ *is 31 . . . * Most of the words the bailiff spoke held no meaning for me. Except, that is, for the five numbers that identified my case from all the other children in foster care.

$4+9=13+9=22+9+0$ *is 31* . . . To calm my nerves, to allow the story of Miss Kerr and me to come through, I added the numbers that identified my case together:

$4+9=13+9=22+9+0$ *is 31* . . . I let myself believe that in that moment, there was no number in the world more powerful than the number 31.

All I would have to do is chant it repeatedly—$4+9=13+9=22+9+0$ *is 31*—and somehow God's power would be released to me. I would use it as I pleased. Couldn't everyone in that courtroom see that the number 31 turned around became 13? That was the day I'd met Miss Kerr. She'd been the one to say, "Look, today is your birthday." I didn't know my birthday from any other day.

"Is there anything you'd like to say on your behalf, young lady?"

The judge spoke from behind a tan desk. A podium and a long-necked microphone separated me from his face.

"I want to live with Miss Kerr." I said. The judge shuffled through some papers, then glanced over at Gwen Forde.

"Counselor, who is Miss Kerr?" the judge asked Gwen.

"Your Honor, may I approach the bench?" Gwen asked.

She walked over to the judge and handed him papers in a file.

Silence.

"I am to understand that this Miss Kerr is a counselor at the Edgar Children's Shelter, where you are currently being detained?"

"Yeah."

"Okay, thank you," the judge said, closing the file.

"Bailiff, now, will you please escort minor from the courtroom."

The bailiff slanted his hand beside me and led me from the podium, down the short aisle, into the courthouse hallway.

I sat on a bench outside the courtroom doors and waited for Gwen.

Shortly thereafter the judge made his decision.

Before I realized I'd left Martinez

I'd arrived at Guideways just as the leaves started to fall in late September, and I was nearly sixteen and a half.

Guideways was a Level 14 residential treatment center fully equipped to handle the emotionally charged disturbances of adolescent girls. Its staff could provide psychotropic medication support. The team at Guideways was going to rehabilitate my behavior. It was supposed to be "a last-ditch effort" before I was, as threatened yet again, shipped off to the Napa State Hospital adolescent ward.

They had a wing for children like me at Napa State, I had learned, children who were beyond the reach of psychological interventions like talk therapy and behavior-modification programs. The joke was that kids like me forced everyone who worked with us to become emotionally exhausted; thus, it was questionable if we were worth the effort it would take to save us.

Gwen Forde pulled her white county car into the slot marked Visitor and ordered me out of the car. She popped all four door locks at once, setting my heart racing. I was a sprinter stuck in my starting block, going nowhere fast.

I wished her luck getting me to move.

All I could think about

I sat in that white county car and thought back to the last time I saw Miss Kerr, right after that court date. I thought about how I had run to the girls' section, needing to find her, about how I'd heard someone yell at me to stop running, but their words fell flat behind me. About how I had rounded the corner and heard someone crying. Hard. It was a grown-woman kind of sound, loud and unrestrained, as opposed to that of a girl who hadn't yet learned the landscape, or weight, of her own grief. I thought about how I had crossed the doorway leading from the long hall that separated the boys' section from the girls', the main office from the living quarters, and into the dining area. About how I'd found Miss Kerr, lying on the kitchen floor, her legs drawn up close to her chest as though she were a small child. Oh, how she yowled, and how it gripped hold of me, not letting me go. It took mere seconds for me to get across the room, and kneeling beside her, I thought about how when I'd asked her what the matter was, she'd said:

"I . . . tried . . . to make you . . . my daughter, today."

When

"When will I get to see Miss Kerr again?" I asked Gwen. "You're just plain hateful, Regina," Gwen said, and pulled the key from the ignition. That's not what I needed to hear.

"Why don't you ask me what *I* want?" I asked. I was no longer afraid of Gwen. Once I realized she didn't *really* like me, that she didn't *really* want what was best for me, and that she couldn't put her hands on me, I also realized I could say just about anything I wanted to her.

"C'mon and do it!" I screamed.

"Do it! Ask me what I want!" I let the rage of her snatching from me the only something I felt was mine settle in between us.

"*Ask me*: What do you want, Regina?" I interrupted the silence.

"Fine then. I'll ask myself," I said. Gwen already thought I was crazy; what harm would a little more of the same do?

"What do *you* want, Regina?" I asked out loud.

"What is it that you want?"

"I want to walk down the street with Miss Kerr. I want to reach for her hand to thread my fingers through hers and swing our arms back and forth, up and over, back and forth, up and over, churning forever down, down into our bones. I want to be like any other girl black or white or whatever color girls come in. Secretly, I want to know what it might feel like to call Miss Kerr *Mama*."

A whole lot of "ifs"

"Bravo!" Gwen replied, clapping. "If that's all you want, Regina, to get back with your little white friend, then you'll need to show me something a lot more than that crazy-show you just put on. You can fool the psychiatrist and your white-lady friend, but you don't fool me." Gwen stepped out of the car, grabbed her briefcase, and slammed the door. She walked around to my side. I sat there. I was worn out from the heat, the almost-three-hour drive with traffic, the heaviness of yet another blowup with Gwen, and the reality of yet another placement: more girls to get to know, more stories about their messed-up families, more eyes to echo back to me what I didn't have, and what I probably wasn't *ever* going to have, according to Gwen. More staff members, doctors, rules, ways I needed to act . . .

"If you don't want me to write up an incident report of verbal assault, I suggest you start rethinking how to speak to me," Gwen threatened as she yanked the passenger door open. "Get. Out. Of. My. Car. Now!"

I'd never seen Gwen so hyped up.

"And another thing: if you don't get out, I will call back-up and make it so that you don't see the inside of another car for the rest of your time in care." Uncertain whether she could make that happen, or what that even meant, I stepped out of the car. Gwen popped the trunk. I grabbed hold of my garbage bag and started toward the building.

Just as we stepped up to the front door of Guideways, Gwen turned and said, in a voice I had to strain to make out, "If you *ever* want to see your precious Miss Kerr again, I suggest you make this placement stick like vanilla to ice cream. That is your favorite flavor, right? Vanilla?"

As a child, I never understood the digs that Gwen seemed so inclined to make at my expense. I couldn't name it back then—specifically—the feeling that came over me whenever I was around her. She seemed hell-bent on pushing me toward the edge of having a distaste for my own skin color; I was becoming afraid of it, afraid of myself. I felt like I wasn't okay being just who I was. That there was a secret way to being black—her kind of black—and she was downright aggravated that I didn't know the rules, so as punishment for my ignorance, she made it clear that I wasn't good enough to join her club, only deserving of her jabs.

Gwen had every opportunity to educate me to the ways she wanted me to be, if that's in fact what she wanted. She could've given me books to get me up to speed on what it meant to be black—her kind of black. She could've told me stories about her family and the ways they did things, their customs and values and how they interpreted and played out their version of what it meant to be black. Not only would her inclusion potentially assist in healing my *apparent* gap in cultural identity, but it also could've kept me abreast of what was happening in other black folks' lives. Didn't she know before she placed me in Redding, California, two hours and forty-eight minutes away from another black person, that my being surrounded by the very people she accused me of impersonating only aided and abetted in erasing my barely-hanging-by-a-thread sense of blackness? She could've told me about the politics of the Black Panthers, the importance of Black Power, and the struggle these movements were addressing; she could have helped me understand the importance of connecting my sense of individual identity to that of a broader, more inclusive one.

Back then, I may not have known what her big words meant, or understood the revulsion beneath the cockeyed looks Gwen would give me, but one thing was clear: Gwen had very little tolerance for the child I was, and her only interest seemed to lie in the child she wished me to be.

I wonder if the shame and humiliation I carried back then was due to the hard-won misdeeds that earned me the reputation of being difficult, or perhaps in some perverted act of self-hatred, were compounded by Gwen's unresolved matters concerning her own identity. I didn't know it back then, that both Gwen and I possessed the same bullying qualities. I took my rage and jealousy about not being wanted out on the children who had what I didn't; this gave me a false sense of superiority, the only way for me to have power over someone else, to control something. I always felt guilty after I committed my acts of violence, always made a way to say that I was sorry. I don't ever remember Gwen acknowledging the pain she caused me. It was as though she felt entitled to do so. Perhaps, like the kids I terrorized after school, for Gwen I, too, was an easy target.

The rules

We weren't supposed to: touch one another, or sit so close that body contact became an arguable matter; borrow anyone else's personal belongings, as in socks, underwear, toothbrushes, clothing, shampoo, or prescribed medications; further escalate an already escalating situation, make comments, or express emotional frustration in the television room or any other room where residents were likely to gather, such as the van, the swimming pool area, the kitchen, or at the dining room table; receive mail, care packages, love letters, letters of concern from a family member, a friend, an ex-counselor, previous staff we may've had a relationship with prior to our residency at Guideways who had not been revetted and therefore not placed on our "call lists" (it did not matter if our social workers knew the person(s) before we arrived, and it did not matter if said person already had established evidence of a "positive connection"); leave the grounds without a staff escort, also known as being absent without leave (AWOL); attend any school we wanted to, outside activities, social excursions, personal occasions, or anything that would require a judge's decision; apply for after-school jobs, or audition at local community center theater productions for the opportunity to try on a dream of one day becoming an actor, singer, anything; have our dreams taken seriously.

We would need to earn our way onto level one and keep it for the duration of one month before earning the privilege to: smoke cigarettes, call one person who'd been approved on our call list, go for rides in the van with staff to the local 7-Eleven, do extra chores for extra money to purchase cigarettes. We would need to earn level two to go to the mall with a purchase order to Sears & Roebuck or J.C. Penney, with a staff member in tow. We would need to earn level three to have our own room, a full closet, a shared bathroom, and the right to have other residents visit our rooms without staff supervision. We weren't allowed to: have sex on or off the property; have alcohol or drugs; attend any friends' parties, homes, gatherings. We weren't allowed to make friends, have them over for popcorn and a movie on a Friday or Saturday night, without a judge's decree. We were only allowed to occupy the chronological ages of our respective childhoods, but not the joys of freedom that went along with that. Our stories were sifted through therapeutic frameworks that reordered our existences and stranded us on the other side of our inalienable right to pursue happiness. We were segregated from ourselves, like hazardous waste, rendered less than ordinary trash.

Touch me

On a blisteringly hot Saturday night, a solid month of successfully abiding by the Guideways rules—doing it their way—beneath my belt, I sat in Lola's room on the edge of her bed, my eyes closed as she drew cool water into the small bathtub at the opposite end of the room. She was one of the residents who'd played by the rules and earned level three faster than anyone else ever had. Which meant she'd scored her own room, her own schedule, and relationships with staff, who seemed to bend to her will.

It was her choice that I come and "hang out" in her room, "just the two of us," while most of the other girls, along with the staff, were out for a night of roller skating at the local rink. It was Lola's night to wash her hair and she "sure as hell wasn't going to hang with any of them country-bunk girls" who stayed drugged and lifeless. She'd seen me plait another resident's hair and had commented on how quickly my fingers moved in and out of the dense mass.

I'd learned to braid hair in a dream when I was eleven or so. My sister, who was born braiding hair and did so with the quickness of a humming-bird, had refused to teach me. So, I'd watched her. My eyes recorded each move she made at the speed she made it, and in my dreams, I'd slow her fingers down and replace them with my own. When I awoke, I asked my sister if I could braid her hair, and like that, I was able to. I learned most everything like that.

Lola's daddy had her move into her mother's side of his bed when her mama died, or was it that her mama ran off with another man? Memory can sometimes be so elusive. Either way, her leaving left a vacancy. She became her daddy's second wife in every manner of the word *wife*. This quick-started Lola into an adulthood few if any of us girls could handle, and when that half-black, half-Japanese girl, whose long black hair brushed the curve of her spine when she walked, lowered those eyes the shape of teardrops tilted toward heaven, all I could do was whatever she told me to. I'd always had an inclination for the beauty of girls, their rituals.

I was a tomboy. Rough. A bull in a china cabinet. Rarely remembered to lotion my skin, change my underwear, brush my teeth, wash my hair. Bathe, even. I saw myself more like a black-girl version of Huckleberry Finn. Always afraid I'd miss something, I took as little time as possible for *me*. I needed to be in the mix, know what was going on; I was always solving for not being left behind. I imagined there were things Lola could show me if I were to move up through the behavior-mod system at Guideways. I heard her break the water's surface in the bathtub and I opened my eyes, and tried hard not to let them fall upon her nakedness, for fear that somehow, I'd see my own and blush with secret embarrassment.

But when Lola said, "Get on over here, girl, and cool my back off," I thought not about refusing her, or what might happen if someone found out, but rather, I thought of what it would feel like to touch another human being, a girl whose skin was four shades deeper than my own, which made her the Reese's Peanut Butter Cup chocolate outside to my peanut-butter center. These things together reminded me of my sister, who was the same color as Lola, and someone I'd shared a bed with, the two of us stuck together like stacked chairs, up until I'd left Texas five years prior. I yearned for a bit of both: the spooning and my sister.

The penalty for an infraction—touching, for instance—involved the loss of privileges and a possible level demotion, depending on who committed the infraction and how many warnings they'd already been given. If found out, the wrongdoer would have to do a few extra chores to earn back the lost privileges. I'd earned level one, and still hadn't received permission to call Miss Kerr. I took the sponge Lola offered.

My buttocks rested on the lip of the tub and I waited. Watched. Lola twisted her hair into a chignon that sat upon her head, crown-like. With both hands, I squeezed the heavy sponge and let the water run the length of her smooth skin again and again. I scrubbed her back tenderly, as if she were my own child, as if I loved her. I picked up the bar of Ivory soap, and painted her hair with it. My fingers dug deep into her hair, felt the shape of her head. For a minute I was lost in the ritual, lost in the touching that seemed to help me remember once again what it felt like to be human, to be kind and useful, to be needed.

I was taken back to South Austin. My fascination with girls' rituals started there with Trinity Rodriguez. I'd wait till after school to fight kids. Propelled by an impulse to impersonate Catwoman, I'd jump them from behind a bush, a garbage can, a tree. Trinity intervened one day when I targeted her friend; she stood up to me and offered to become my friend if I spared her friend. I accepted. Over time, given that I was sent home earlier than the other students, to give me a head start and spare them the brunt of my misplaced rage, Trinity agreed to leave the key to her house for me in a tear in her brother's motorcycle seat.

The ritual: I'd go to her house and do as she instructed—remove my clothes and hide. Sometimes I'd hide in a closet, or beneath a bed. Trinity would arrive home and start searching for me. Maybe I'd allow her to go past me before I ran from cover and forced a chase, only to outrun her. We'd wear ourselves thin, changing the rules as we went. I loved the rule of whichever one of us found the other first, got to do whatever she wanted. I was much faster than Trinity so it was easy for me to get to the designated safety area first. And I came to prefer her catching me. That way, if God were watching, the things we did would be her fault, not mine. Trinity taught me how to touch her breasts, and the outsides of our vaginas. Sometimes, the sensations the touching unleashed hypnotized me for days. It was the first time I felt what my insides felt: mouthwateringly delicious. A pillow between us, we'd grind our narrow hips into one another, and kissed using our tongues as though we were both morphing into the whole being of the other. This ritual became one of my favorite pastimes. Sometimes I got into trouble just so that Trinity would chastise me. Gently. After, Trinity would clean herself up, remove any traces that I'd been there, that we'd *been* there.

Loss

It was one thing to learn that Gwen wouldn't be attending my one-month review meeting, which would acknowledge my success at Guideways, and another to hear that she'd "lost one of her kids." I didn't know that Gwen was married! And a child out of wedlock? Never. I probed deeper, and asked Phyllis, the in-house social worker who'd delivered the news, why she thought Gwen had never let on that she had a kid.

Turns out, Gwen didn't have any children of her own. Apparently, she saw the children on her caseload as *hers* and we were enough for her. I was correct: she was not married. Gwen had lost a boy, classified as a juvenile delinquent, fourteen, to a car accident. He'd stolen the car, driven too fast, and the car got away from him. He crashed. DOA.

That was the first time I'd had a chance to envision Gwen as human. In my own heart, I felt the sadness she must've felt the instant she'd heard the news, her eyes suddenly moist with grief. I imagined that, like me, every now and again she'd had lunch with him, the deceased one, and maybe she had moments when she was kind to him. Also, I imagined she might be the only one who'd attend his funeral, send him off with a handful of flowers. Blue. Carnations.

That day, the one where I learned about Gwen's loss, I also heard that even given how well I'd done, attaining level one and keeping it, and how I really knew how to become a "joiner" and how refreshing that was, still the staff thought it might be best if I try and maintain my status for another month. "It'll be a piece a cake for you," Phyllis said. I swallowed my disbelief. "It'll be a piece of cake," she said. Moving the finish line was not the way to maintain trust. I'd had to wait an entire month to make that call, to receive a call. I'd given them what they wanted. I was not walking away from that, not going to become demotivated. With all due respect, I wanted what was mine, what I'd worked for, so I asked if I could *finally* call Miss Kerr. It was my turn.

I made no dramatic outburst. I did not curse at Phyllis or tell her that her teeth looked like tiny Chiclets, which made it difficult to pay attention to anything she'd say because I was far too busy twisting my head this way and that trying to count her teeny-tiny teeth. I did not bust a move and throw papers and overturn chair and desks and act like the white girls who got away with crazy on the daily. I did not kick the shit out of the file cabinets and empty garbage cans, and wild out as I watched Phyllis root through my file, pull out my call list, and say: "She's not here. Jeanne Kerr is not on your approved call list."

There was no name on my call list except one: Gwen Forde.

S.c.h.e.h.e.r.a.z.a.d.e.

School at Guideways was considered *on grounds*, but each day the residents packed into a brown 1978 Econoline van and were driven to an abandoned elementary school that had been reconstituted as a school for "severely emotionally disturbed" girls which, of course, was the label affixed to my skin like an out-of-style leisure suit: I was tired of wearing it. We were called SEDs for short.

Guideways School had several modular buildings that were situated around an asphalt basketball court. There was a typical schoolyard metal merry-go-round, bolted into the asphalt, near the basketball court. Someone would have to grab one of the bars, get a running start while pushing on the bar, and then jump on and ride until either we became so light-headed we had to get off, or the motion stopped and then somebody would have to start the whole push, run, jump, and ride sequence all over again. And there was a lone tetherball pole surrounded by what felt like acres of uneven asphalt.

By then, it had been a few years since I'd attended school. So much time was lost waiting for previous records to come from wherever they were last shipped to. Many times, I'd flee the placement before the records ever reached their destination. What I remembered about school and what I looked forward to were PE and writing—but I liked shopping for school supplies and clothes most of all. I loved the yellow Ticonderoga #2 pencils, and how their lead could hold a point; I loved the smell of the plastic see-through pen and pencil holder with the top zipper; and I loved the spiral notebooks and the way each page was cut and ruled perfectly on each side, though many times I wrote far beyond the margins. I always needed more room.

The deal, however, about being a ward of the court was that everything had to go through a process of approval. And it wasn't until a request from a resident was made known to a counselor, or a therapist, that a purchase order was then drafted, the amount agreed upon, the order signed, then handed over to a social worker, who'd send it off to the facility manager, who'd discuss its pending arrival to the resident each day, until finally—usually months later—in a meeting, the manager would divulge that the requested PO had arrived, and then the mostly disinterested parties might debate who was going to take the resident who had made the request to the mall. By then, at least for me, the thrill of starting school would have passed.

I became motivated by a series of lessons in a box. These boxes were categorized by subject: math, social studies, history, literature, theater. Once inside the classroom, we'd take our seats, and after the teacher did a head count, we were expected to go to the box of the subject we'd left off from the day before. My aim was to finish an entire grade level as quickly as I could to stay on track for college.

Once, I'd discussed college as an option with Gwen, and the look she gave me would've rivaled the blob fish—the ugliest fish alive. But it was already in my body, going to college was, and there was nothing Gwen could do to take that from me. I was already feeling the somebody I knew I would one day be; I just needed time to come into myself, that was all.

Apparently, my love for books had begun when I was three or four years old. I don't know the full chronology of how I learned to read, but I do know that I always read books, broke bread with books (or bags of Fritos corn chips to be exact), and on many a night I slept with my books, right there beneath my pillow, and sometimes inside the pillowcase.

It was Miss Kerr who'd told me to "never skip over a word you don't know." I still had the dictionary/thesaurus she'd given me as a going-away present. Though we'd never said *goodbye*.

So, by the time I'd made it through the sixth-, seventh-, eighth-, ninth-, and tenth-grade boxes, I'd read about the Constitution of the United States, had every word of its preamble memorized, and understood the differences between *ascribe* and *attain* well enough to envision that I could—one day—be more than what I was born into (ascribed), if I was willing to work for it (attain).

Then I found the story of Scheherazade and *The Arabian Nights*. I couldn't stop reading, and falling in love with how one girl, because of everything that she had studied and all that she had remembered, was able to save her own life, transform a killing machine of a king, and become queen. If Scheherazade could do that, so could I. For months, I read everything I could get my hands on. I also demanded that everyone around me call me Scheherazade. "S.c.h.e.h.e.r.a.z.a.d.e." Scheherazade I would be.

The file

The file cabinet containing all the case files of the residents' histories was kept in the on-site psychiatrist's office. Morris was his name. The cabinet remained locked. At all times. Morris took the key with him each night after work. A hundred times I'd watched him sit back in his armchair, one leg across the other, twirling his pencil between his lip and moustache. Sometimes, he'd rock back and forth. I'd speak. He'd jot something down, I'd speak. He'd jot something down. Once, I asked, "What are you writing about me?" I was curious. I had spent more time being analyzed than I had playing dress up, or flirting with boys, or dreaming about a regular life of a husband, a house, two children, maybe even a dog.

"Just a few notes," Morris replied. I knew better than to believe him.

"Can I read what you wrote about me?" I was serious. "I don't know, *can you?*" He thought himself quite funny. I thought him quite stupid.

Lola had confided in me that Morris might be persuaded to see things "my way" if I were willing to come off as nicey-nice. Karo-syrupy-like. All I'd have to do was compliment him on a body part. Apparently, Morris had a hang-up about the front of his hair, the way you could see straight through it to the back of his head, so to say to him, "Man, your hair is blazin' today, Morris," could've made things he wrote down go my way. But playing nice hadn't delivered me the phone call I'd earned.

Cabinet

It was a busy Monday, two days after I'd learned about Gwen's challenges and that I didn't have anyone on my call list, when Lola asked for the screwdriver to tighten the screws on her window shades. Once done, she'd followed procedure and placed the tool back into the custodian's basket, and signed it in again on the clipboard that hung on the wall in the counselor's office. I slipped in right behind her and grabbed the screwdriver before anyone had time to take it back to the toolshed, log it in, and lock it up.

I half expected someone to have seen me, to have sat all day on the fact that I'd not only stolen something, I'd done worse: I'd stolen something that belonged to the facility. I told myself that I was being watched, and that whoever it was, was biding their time to narc on me, watch me get busted, only to laugh their maddening laugh all while getting hyped on the spectacle of it all. But nothing like that happened.

A little while before midnight, and at least forty-five minutes before the night-shift workers handed over the keys to the graveyard worker, Edith, I stood in front of the beige file cabinet in Morris's office. I was stealth. The bathroom window had been left unlocked. Lucky for me. I'd planned on breaking it anyway, with a knee-high basketball sock over my hand, Mafia style.

I placed the head of the screwdriver between the cabinet lock bar and a partially opened drawer. I pulled until the drawer pulled away from its casing enough for me to see the files hanging on the glider. It was too easy finding my name. I was the only resident whose last name ended with O.

I read a brief letter from a social worker I didn't remember:

Dear Gwen Forde, MSW:

I am following up on the conversation we had about Regina. As I hand this case off to you I want to summarize a few thoughts. I agree that a residential placement sounds like the best approach, now.

Because Regina has poor internal control, a firm, well-defined, and consistent structure is most helpful to her. She responded best when the limits were clearly known to her and were enforced.

Besides this type of structure, Regina has strong, unmet dependency needs. She sees herself as having made all the decisions about her various living circumstances, i.e., with her foster grandmother, in Texas; her mother, whereabouts unknown; and her father, who resides in Richmond, California, but refuses to maintain contact with his daughter.

Therefore, she feels responsible for many of the unpleasant circumstances in her life. Regina has a need for a great amount of adult attention, and she needs a space to calm her inner life apart from the pressures of group living. Furthermore, consistency and firmness in limit-setting gives her the security that she is cared for.

███████████████

Social Worker
November 18, 1976

The psychological report from Dr. Cohen started out:

December 18, 1978

████████████████████

███████████████

El Cerrito, CA, 94530

███████

Patient, a young black female, possibly beautiful, arrived this afternoon, to my office, for her appointment in a timely manner. There was no noticeable evidence of a patois, and upon further inquiry I found that patient presented, dialectically, as well as could be expected considering she is a Negro girl of a particular background.

Patient (16), arrived dressed in tight-fitting black jumpsuit with bell-bottoms, which accentuated her body, possibly suggesting a peculiar type of sensuality: one such that might be expected from a woman ten years the senior of patient's age.

Although patient exhibited behaviors consistent with someone who is intent on seduction or charm, I do not believe her intent was either to seduce, or charm . . .

I raced and read at the pace of my heartbeat and could not keep up. My fingers ran over the tops of pages clamped together with staples and large paper clips, each packed to the margins with words that had very little meaning for me at that time: Borderline Personality Disorder, Oppositional Disorder, Immaturity Disorder. Manic-Depressive. All labels meant to further marginalize and isolate me from a much-needed healing. One that could never be accomplished by mitigating my essence to nothing more than a pathology worthy of being cured, or fixed, my hopes and dreams neutered.

I didn't know exactly *what* I was looking for, but I knew I was running out of time and I wanted to find out what Morris had to say about me. I wanted to know if he was talking smack behind my back, telling lies. And then I found a Xerox copy of a letter:

October 12th, 1978

Dear Punkin!

I'm sending this letter to you through Gwen Forde. I pray that things are well with you, that you are, as you said, doing your very best and letting the people at Guideways get to know you—showing them the Regina I know and LOVE!

Regina, it will be up to you how you adjust at Guideways, which will determine when you will hear from me again. Many people who also care about you have told me that it will make it hard for you to adjust and settle in if we keep writing, talking, and seeing each other until you have established roots in your new home. I'm counting on you to let yourself settle in and do your very best to let this placement work. Those old key words: It's up to you honey. Until I am given permission I will not write you nor will I accept any phone calls and I will not see you. You know, Punkin, a period of silence and separation is a very small part of time when you look at a lifetime. I know with all my heart that we will be close friends our whole life long. I am behind you, Punkin, rooting for you all the way.

Some things we must face alone, but I am always with you in spirit. You are always in my heart. You need to discuss things with your social worker, share your thoughts and feelings, confide in the staff there, and make new friendships.

As you said, "Think about your actions," and the consequences of those actions before you act. Do your very best to work on those basics, sweetheart. It doesn't happen overnight; have patience. Each day is a new start, a new beginning. You may have to start new each day. I have faith in you; if you put your mind to it and keep plugging away it will eventually happen.

One suggestion is to each night ask yourself if you have done your very best that day; see where changes can be made, and then try again. It takes concentration and willpower; you can do it if you really want to!

Another suggestion is to ask yourself what nice thing you have done for someone else that day. You are very good at this, it's one of your special qualities that make you, YOU!

I keep remembering that you are in God's hands; the very best hands, and that you have decided to settle in, and do your very best. Once you put your mind and will behind something, Regina, and you do your very best, the rest is up to God. Trust Him, Regina; He loves you more than anyone.

With All My Love,

Jeanne K. Kerr

Ms. J.K. Kerr

If you'd like to make a call, please hang up, and try again

The pay phone in the residents' TV room was anchored to the wall straight across from the counselor's office. I'd forgotten how long I'd been in Morris's office reading through the file, forgotten to take note of when I heard the wheels of Edith's cherried-out El Camino spit gravel as it made a ninety-degree turn into the driveway, forgotten to close the file cabinet. Forgotten to think to bring change with me to make the call I believed I'd earned.

In the counselor's office, receiver in hand, I dialed Jeanne's number.

"Miss Kerr? It's me, Regina." She'd picked up on the third ring.

"Hi sweetheart," she said, groggily. "What time is it? Are you okay?"

Barely able to contain myself, I cupped my hand over my mouth and the receiver.

"When're you coming to see me?"

"Do you have permission to speak with me, Regina?"

"Why haven't you called?"

"It's after 2 a.m."

"Are you coming—"

"Sweetheart, I can't talk with you."

"I gotta know when you're coming."

"I have to go, sweetie. I'm . . . sorry."

SHU

Later that morning.

Hands the size of a Rawlings catcher's mitt, at the end of arms thick as bologna logs. The unit aide gripped my wrist and ankle, digging his nails into my flesh, squeezing and kneading until it felt as if I were going to pop right out of me. With back-and-forth motions he pulled me from my bed, out of my room, and down the hallway, using my body to sweep away everything in our path: rugs, chairs, and forgotten-about shoes. I knew where we were going.

I was a windshield wiper. He was a restraining staff member committed to enforcing the rules. We tripped over the plastic tables, where the rest of the residents sat with sunken faces, falling in at the mouth from eating watery powdered eggs and cold Wonder Bread.

"What are y'all looking at?" I yelled. He swung me. We do-si-doed.

"I can call anybody I want, man!"

The way the other residents sat there, not helping, with nothing staring back at me from inside their sunken eyes, reminded me of old people in a convalescent home.

I'd earned that phone call.

That dumb-ass song from *Mister Rogers' Neighborhood* wafted from the bulging eye of the Zenith TV, as Fatman raked my body across the floor tiles, their splintered and chipped edges so sharp that nobody's bare feet were safe, let alone my legs dangling from shorts.

I imagined chunks of reddish-brown pieces of me spackled into the places where the tiles used to be. No matter how hard I tried, that day was not going to be a beautiful one in my neighborhood.

"I earned that call, man!"

"Forget y'all! I ain't going in there!"

"I ain't going." Fatman kept hauling me through the room.

"I didn't ask to come here in the first place," I screamed, struggling against his strength. I tore at him, the plastic checkered tabletop, and the plates that crashed to the floor, trying to hold on to something. Anything. I grabbed at someone's leg. She kicked my hands off her. Went back to eating.

I became slippery with food and sweat from kicking and fighting. Fatman let go of my arm long enough to lift a silver gym-teacher whistle to his lips and blow.

I flipped around and sank my teeth into his calf. He howled. He was a wounded beast. Game changed.

"We've got a biter! Need back-up NOW!" Fatman screamed into the two-way radio he'd pulled from his hip. Somebody should've told him. He pulled back. Too late. I was a rabid dog who wasn't about to let go of him. They'd have to kill me first.

Startled, he kicked and batted at the air. But, like a pit bull, I sank my jaw deeper into him. With the sticky palm of his hand he smashed down on the side of my face. His fingers pried into my lips, clawed my gums, my teeth, my grip.

Fatman screamed and danced around as far as his free leg would allow him to move, then toppled to the ground. Someone wound my plaited hair around their hand and jerked me from behind, while another somebody bum-rushed their entire hand inside my mouth.

My head yanked back, my jaw unlocked, Fatman cried out like a kicked-in-the-belly bitch. Through the splay of fingers, I watched him palm-and-slide, palm-and-slide his fatness all the way down the hall, out of my sight.

A staff person we called Maryanne the Yes Man had her arm around my throat, in a choke hold. I tried to kick my way out of it, but she dragged me down anyway. I flailed and she snatched my black self down a flight of twenty-two stairs. I lost a footie, the one with the yellow pom-pom on the back, the one Miss Kerr had given me, and I couldn't get loose. Breath was hard to come by. Somebody grabbed my feet, foot-cuffed them, and wheelbarrowed me forward and down. Down to the last step.

I knew what was coming. I knew where they were taking me. I'd seen many girls fold themselves into embryos for days after being released from the security-housing unit. I'd heard that once inside the SHU box, all hell was going to break loose. Once inside, there'd be no coming out until I could "learn to self-soothe." Once inside, there would be no me. No God. I would not remember how to recite John 3:16.

Maryanne the Yes Man barked at someone to "open the door!"

"I'll be good now!" I screamed. "Good! Just don't put me in there. Please, don't!" Five, six, maybe even seven sets of hands pushed me into a room no bigger than a burying plot. A blurry group of gowns and pajamas crowded the stairwell. "Back to your rooms NOW!" Maryanne the Yes Man yelled.

"I'm going to die in here," I cried, and tried to ram past the staff members' bodies that blocked the doorway. They held on to one another's torsos and shoulders. They wove a thick net.

"I'm going to die," I said and continued to push against the hands, arms, and legs that jammed my only way out. I rammed hard. Hard against them. Hard against them.

Someone pushed back with such force I was knocked onto the wooden floor. I scrambled to get up onto my hands and knees in time to reach for the door as it slammed shut. It barely missed my fingertips.

"I . . . can't breathe." I pounded with both hands. "Somebody, HELP ME!"

"You'll get as good as you get. Now bring it down, way down!"

There was no handle. No windows. No air. The ceiling plunged toward me. The walls pressed in. My fingernails scraped against the floor.

I was slipping and sliding like a dog on hardwood floors. There was nothing to hold on to. I wanted to vomit and catch my breath all at once. Although my body trembled, I scrambled down into the space where door and baseboard meet. I opened my mouth to scream into the slit of light barely showing through, but everything was upside down. I needed air, I sucked, and sucked, and sucked for air, wishing, hoping, wanting my own mother.

"Ruby . . ."

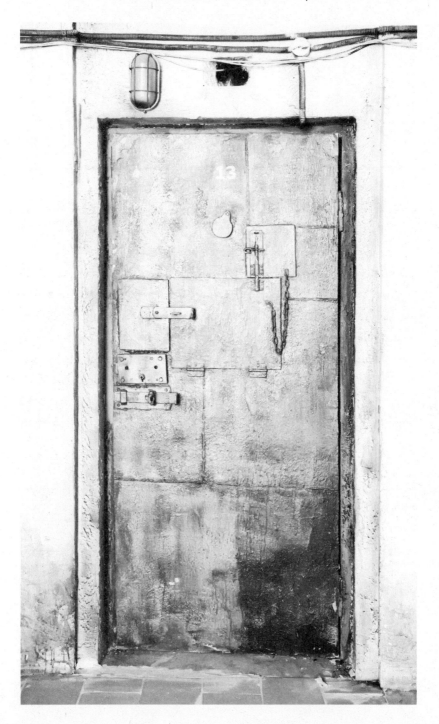

Antipsychotic

"Next," the nurse called out. In two months' time I'd messed myself up good: from being the first to get my chores done, to get into the van, the pool, the line for dinner, to being the last in line to throw back bitter-tasting meds from a tiny, white, pleated Dixie cup.

The nurse. Morris. Phyllis. Gwen. All the adults who oversaw my care made it their business to convince me that my destructive behavior was not my fault. They told me that my body had deficiencies that wouldn't allow my brain to function normally, like "regular" kids my age. I was told that to stay at Guideways, and not be terminated or transferred to a low-level psychiatric ward for adolescents, I'd have to agree to a daily regime of psychotropic meds. Most all the residents, except Lola, relied upon one cocktail after another of prescribed medications to aid them in getting through the day.

I didn't want the meds. I took the meds because I didn't want to end up relying on prescription drugs to make it through my life, and I figured if I took them then, I'd fix whatever was broken inside me.

I had dreams. I was good with hair, I had vocals, I was told I was runway-model pretty. I saw how people stared at me when I entered a room, how they smiled. I made those interactions matter; I let them let me feel good about me. I imagined myself a ballet dancer. It always ran through my mind what Miss Kerr had said: "You can become anything you want."

I would always believe her.

Day after day I popped two small orange Thorazine pills. Then I popped two small brown Mellaril pills. Then I popped a small pink Stelazine pill. Then I popped a large peach capsule of Thorazine. If taken according to prescription, the Thorazine, Mellaril, and Stelazine were meant to alleviate adverse behaviors, and any traces or symptoms of mental illness I may have had. I was diagnosed as schizophrenic one minute, and manic the next, bipolar on Monday, and histrionic by Friday. Up and down it went, my diagnosis.

No one explained to me, back then, what *good* behavior looked like on the medication. Therefore, it was difficult for me to know what to watch for. What I *understood* fully, was that my soul ached on the daily to be touched, caressed, and held. I wanted to attend cookouts and family reunions (even if they weren't my family), like I had from time to time at Big Mama's. I dreamt of attending the theater with Miss Kerr, of having a pen pal in a faraway country I'd visit one day, once I was grown-up. I could have been a track star. I was fast. Real fast. I wanted someone to explain things to me in a language that made sense; in other words, I wanted to be let in on my own life, given entrance and access to me and what was happening and why it seemed the people I loved and wanted, clearly, didn't feel the same way about me.

Lithium bicarbonate was in a class all its own. Lithium is what's used when other antidepressants have failed. It reduces the risk of suicide.

Cup of pills

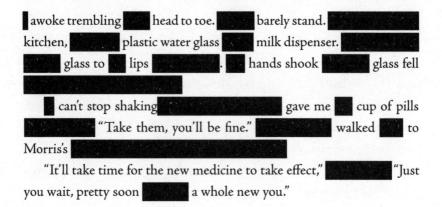

█ awoke trembling ███ head to toe. ████ barely stand. ██████████
kitchen, ███████ plastic water glass ███ milk dispenser. ████████
██████ glass to █ lips ██████████. █ hands shook ███████ glass fell
████████████████████████

████ can't stop shaking████████████████ gave me █ cup of pills
█████████ "Take them, you'll be fine." ████████████████ walked ███ to
Morris's ████████████████████████████████

   "It'll take time for the new medicine to take effect," ████████████ "Just
you wait, pretty soon ████████ a whole new you."

Weeks later

Another hot day at Guideways. Morris and Phyllis thought it was a good idea for me to get out of the house, get an "airing out," they'd called it. I'd gone through a series of repeated hospital visits where I'd had to be injected with Cogentin to counteract shitting myself, swallowing my tongue, losing control of my tongue, hand, and limbs. Sometimes these spells were preceded by a lost sense of smell. That was my warning sign.

Swimming would be good for my body, they said. Miss Kerr had taught me to freestyle across the entire length of an Olympic-sized pool at Heather Farms, a public park in Walnut Creek. We'd switch it up between the farm and the Y in Pleasant Hill. For whatever reason, I hadn't readily taken to the pool at Guideways. Perhaps it was the way we had to ask permission each time anyone wanted to swim. Or the annoyance of the eight-foot cyclone fence that traveled the circumference of the pool. It was secured with a padlock the size of a bowling ball, chains layered upon chains that had lost their shine like cheap costume jewelry for the disenfranchised. Then there was that feeling that the pool area was more like a water treatment plant, or an aquarium where we were the freaks people were meant to come and goggle at from a distance, but didn't. It would've been magical had Miss Kerr been there busting cannonballs and jackknives right alongside me, her daringly leading the way, me reluctantly following behind. I'd love the way she'd look me dead in the eye and clap her hands cheering, "C'mon girl, you can do it . . ." She would've made a great Dallas Cowboys cheerleader. They were super famous back then.

That day, I'd swum a few laps when out of nowhere, my entire body began to do things on its own. I became dizzy to the point of disorientation. My heart rate revved from calm to *I think I'm going to die* within seconds. Each attempt to propel my arms simultaneously to get from the six-foot side of the pool to the shallow end resulted in my splashing at the water the way someone with a palsy might. My arms and legs became heavier, slower. The more I tried to warn the staff member watching me that something was not right, the more paralyzed I became. My mind wanted to raise my arms; my arms had other intentions. My tongue quit working. Words slurred. My head twisted on its own until it stuck at a forty-five-degree angle at my left shoulder and stuttered there, forcing my neck muscles to become a crank-bolt wrench, as if I were Linda Blair in *The Exorcist.*

The staff member waved me away.

"Stop being silly," he yelled.

No sooner did my brain transmit to my legs to kick, my arms to thrust or else drown, than it became evident I was already drowning.

I never remembered being pulled from the pool, the whirring sound of the ambulance, the gurney, the machines, the tubes. But I heard the stories of how it took the medic nearly fifteen minutes, a team of emergency-room doctors and nurses another thirty, to figure out that I was not a Parkinson's patient, but instead, a teen who had been overmedicated.

I awoke in a pool of my own bile, urine, and shit. A male nurse grabbed a handful of my butt cheek, pinched it up into a mound of flesh, and shoved a four-inch needle loaded with Cogentin into me. Was it that time or the multitude of times this happened? The memories' sensations have all merged into one self-felt episode.

Within minutes, my tongue, like a retractable vacuum-cleaner cord, slipped back into my mouth. Using the back of my hand, I wiped the slobber-vomit cocktail from the corners of my mouth.

Man

"Man, y'all gotta take me off this mess," I told Morris, Phyllis, Gwen.
"Man, y'all gotta take me off this mess," I told Morris, Phyllis, Gwen.
"Man, y'all gotta take me off this mess," I told Morris, Phyllis, Gwen.
"Man, y'all gotta take me off this mess," I told Morris, Phyllis, Gwen.
"Man, y'all gotta take me off this mess," I told Morris, Phyllis, Gwen.
"Man, y'all gotta take me off this mess," I told Morris, Phyllis, Gwen.
"Man, y'all gotta take me off this mess," I told Morris, Phyllis, Gwen.
"Man, y'all gotta take me off this mess," I told Morris, Phyllis, Gwen.

Each morning, the nurse handed me the tiny, white, pleated Dixie cup and watched me take my meds.

"Man, y'all gotta take me off this mess," I told Morris, Phyllis, Gwen.
"Man, y'all gotta take me off this mess," I told Morris, Phyllis, Gwen.
"Man, y'all gotta take me off this mess," I told Morris, Phyllis, Gwen.

Each morning, the nurse handed me the tiny, white, pleated Dixie cup and watched me take my meds.

"Man, y'all gotta take me off this mess," I told Morris, Phyllis, Gwen.
"Man, y'all gotta take me off this mess."

Each morning, the nurse handed me the tiny, white, pleated Dixie cup and watched me take my meds.

Manic

All anyone had to do was take a minute and calculate the number of times I'd been ambulanced or rushed to the local hospital, where my body would be pumped full of medication to counteract the adverse side effects of yet another failed drug regime, and then pay attention to what those drugs were taking from me: my ability to think for myself; feed, clothe, and wipe myself; the hopefulness that melted into listlessness that hung in strands of slobber from the side of my sagging mouth. The swollen feet and limb joints, the sleepless nights, my wandering the halls, the headaches.

All anyone had to do—and this was the disgrace of it—was unlock those files they kept on me and all those other girls who shuffled around Guideways so far gone we bore the brunt of the cliché: *the lights are on, but nobody's home.* Social workers, judges, and counselors alike could've worked better together to figure out why we had no visitors, no calls, no real friends, and make it a point to help us get peopled up in such a way that grief would have less of a hold on our young hearts, and free us up to play in the fields of our possibilities.

All anyone had to do was imagine me, back then, as an adolescent girl entitled to my pain, my loss, my grief. I was affected by my compounded family traumas formed by generations upon generations of underwhelming existences, by leaving Miss Kerr, by losing my freedoms, my innocence, my childhood.

What about my hopes, my dreams, my want for a mother—and not just any kind of mother, like the ones they constantly threw my way to try on like old hand-me-down dresses, but one who I had something in common with, one who had a vested interest in my future and well-being, one who chose me as I was choosing her, one who wanted me for a daughter as much as I imagined she could be my mother.

All anybody had to do, really, was search into their own hearts, their own experiences with family, acceptance, belonging and togetherness, failure and loss, and imagine for us girls something more dignified, more humane. To imagine something that shifted the blame placed on us victims, who were already too beaten down to crawl back up the barrel of our collective nothingness into an almost certain future of failure. All anybody had to do was approach us from a place of worthiness, accept us in all our flawed humanity because all I—we—wanted was to know what it felt like to give and receive love.

Porgy and Bess

The theater department at Shasta College had placed an ad in a local daily announcing the casting call for a production of *Porgy and Bess*. I knew nothing about Gershwin, his play, or the music, but the ad was clear: they were looking for a black male and a black female between the ages of seventeen and twenty-one to play the parts of Porgy and Bess. I fit that bill. I believed back then that I was the only black person within a 100-mile radius of Redding, California. There were no black counselors, we had no black neighbors, and any time the ambulance or the police showed up at Guideways—which was all too often—none of them were black. I saw no black folks at the mall, or at the Red Lion Hotel restaurant, where we'd devour deep-fried shrimp on the first of the month if the county had paid its boarding-home wage for us on time.

By then, I'd caught wind of the whispers about how I was getting close to emancipating, and I needed to begin thinking about what I was going to do, where I would go. College remained my number-one choice, but I hadn't been able to convince anyone I had what it took to get in, stay there, and graduate. Maybe I could become a singer like my father, or an actress, or a social worker? Not even when I won several hundred dollars from the ladies over at the Redding Junior League, for getting straight As from the reading boxes, did anybody consider that evidence of what lay within me. Those JL ladies didn't know that I wasn't *really* doing real schoolwork, or that a kindergartner could've probably whipped me to the finish with some of those lessons. They were, however, fascinated by the fact that I could write the letter nominating myself to receive that prize money, which came with a year's supply of Coca-Cola. I liked that they liked that I could do that, and so I wanted to do more things like that—win things—to get people's attention.

The way I tended to look at things was: the casting call, like the Junior League contest, was fate's way of leading me to my destiny. It was, maybe, God's way of telling me to get out of Guideways as soon as I could, God's way of saying look above the heads of those who think they know better than you and cast your sights on a future horizon, then name it, claim it, call it by name: *I will be what I see.*

I didn't bother to ask a staff member to give me a lift down to where the auditions were being held. I sneaked out the back door, past the locked pool area, and ran up the hill to the 7-Eleven on Dana Drive. I waited there, leaning on a wall till I saw a lady I thought looked nice enough to thumb a ride from; she had to be young looking, and smile at me when I gave her eye contact for me to trust her automatically. That's what my gut told me and I listened. Several people flat out avoided my gaze. But then a white girl in her twenties smiled back at me when I walked past her as she was getting into her car. She pulled the Volkswagen Bug out of the parking lot and I quickly held my thumb out, and walked backwards in the direction I was headed, praying she was going my way.

I'd heard the horror stories about young girls taking rides, from a car full of men, who were then discovered chopped up, or else never found again. The Zodiac killer was still on the loose then as well. That struck righteous fear in me. But. I was young. Bold. Idealistic. And believed that all I had to do was tell myself to never let something like that happen, to never take rides from strange men. Even though I thought that hitch-hiking was for white people and that maybe the chick wouldn't stop, I kept walking back as she waited for the coast to clear to pull out of the driveway. She stopped.

"What can you sing?" asked one of the two people who sat at a folding table in front of me. The white chick had dropped me off at the local high school—Enterprise, I believe it was. I had no idea that I was supposed to have a song prepared, and the only one I knew by heart was one I'd heard on the radio some time back by Nina Simone. I got through the first verse of "To Be Young, Gifted, and Black," before I was stopped and handed a page of the playscript to take home and learn.

"Have you ever heard of *Porgy and Bess* before?" the casting director asked, and I told him that I hadn't.

"It's okay," he said. "You did great. Are you available for after-school rehearsals?"

"Yes!" I answered. More than anything, I was happy to say yes to something. I marveled at how easy it was. *Yes.*

My *yes* was quickly sucker punched into a *no!* It wasn't *just* because I had sneaked off to audition for the part that I wasn't allowed to have my "Broadway moment"—it was also because no one at Guideways had ever done such a thing.

Milk vat

By the time the green S.E. Rykoff truck (tattooed with the slogan "Eat Out More Often") pulled out from the back of the Guideways kitchen, I'd already saved up enough pills to tranquilize a small herd of bulls.

Each time the nurse handed me the ten, twenty, or fifty milligrams of whatever I was on that day from the paper cup, I'd stuff the capsules into the seams of my gumline, or plant them at the back of my mouth, which remained dry, beneath my tongue. I had accumulated a month's worth of drugs.

I had a plan. I'd worked on it for weeks after the swimming pool incident, after pleading to be taken off the meds. So. Right after the night shift exchanged keys with Edith, the graveyard worker, I snuck out of bed.

I could hear where Edith was, always. Large woman that she was, her thighs audibly crushed the threads of her polyester pull-on slacks when she walked. Once Edith made her rounds to the other side of the facility, I was up. Earlier that day I'd recovered the pills from the throat of the tree stump where I'd buried them. I'd enclosed them in Saran wrap, and for extra security used a red rubber band to prevent them from getting wet and dissolving.

Pills in hand, I tiptoed down the corridor from my bedroom to the kitchen. From my sock, I grabbed hold of the butter knife I'd saved from dinner. I shoved the butt end of the knife into the space between the U-shaped shackle and the body of the padlock.

The door housing the milk vat was always locked. I gave myself ten minutes to pop that lock. It took one. After I'd come up with the idea,

I'd used the money I'd gotten from the Redding Junior League to buy a pack of locks like the ones used in the kitchen. I'd spent the last month practicing how to break the lock.

I placed the deformed lock on the counter. I opened the front of the milk vat. Using the knife, I slit open the top of the gigantic plastic bag, which held a week's worth of milk. I pulled the pills from the waistband of my underwear, unwrapped them, and dumped all thirty capsules into the milk vat from which the entire facility drank.

Spite

Although I never let on to anyone, Edith and I had a thing. Sometimes, when a drug wreaked havoc on my consciousness and I couldn't make sense of where I was or what was going on, I'd sneak out of bed and head over to the counselor's office, where more often than not I found Edith sitting there, smoking a Marlboro Light and talking to her husband, Larry, who had swastikas tattooed all over his skinny arms. He was the Laurel to her Hardy.

He'd said, "Hey there, Jungle Bunny," the first time I met him, when he'd driven Edith by the facility to pick up her paycheck and she'd made the mistake of introducing us. "Next time, Spear Chucker," was how he said goodbye.

I didn't understand—then—that *all things Larry* pointed to bigotry and an in-your-face abhorrence for anyone who wasn't a white supremacist. I would, later, have a phone call with Gwen and ask if I could stay with Edith over a Christmas holiday. I told Gwen that Edith's husband seemed nice enough, although he'd called me interesting names, ones I'd never heard before, but something about them didn't feel quite right, especially when they'd both laughed when he'd said them.

I repeated the names:

Jungle Bunny.

Spear Chucker.

Gwen gave me that "You have got to be f#@&ing kidding me" stare right through the phone line, until I understood what it felt like, once again, to be the dumbest person alive. Unbeknownst to me, I was when it came to racist behaviors. My young and untutored mind made up that beggars couldn't be choosey, or was there an iota of truth in that belief for a child like me?

"What can I do you for?" Edith asked. Her dentures bulged out a bit from her gums and were very evenly cut, like a pair of windup, chattering teeth. I stood in the doorway. I thought about how I would break what I had done to her.

"C'mon, kiddo, spit it out," Edith said.

"I put a month's worth of meds in the milk vat." I liked Edith. I didn't want her or the other residents to suffer any more than they needed to.

Terminated

Me and the latest garbage bag I used (packed with even fewer things than I had upon my arrival at Guideways) sat in the Redding Municipal Airport terminal. I watched as heat angels danced upon the tarmac, playing tricks on my eyes. So much for telling the truth. Anyway, I was hot, but not as hot as I would've been in the TV room at Guideways (which had no air-conditioning), passing time for the next dose of you-aren't-worth-believing-in to be served up in a paper cup. I was satisfied to sit and await the arrival of the Hughes Airwest flight that was going to take me into San Francisco.

Gwen had refused to make the drive to come and pick me up "one more time" from a failed placement I could've made work. Failure was her way of looking at it, not mine. I could see her reasoning that if I was old enough to be so strong-minded as to be self-destructive, I should've been old enough to face the consequences of my actions and walk the shame of my failure alone. I was fine with that. If being shunned was good enough for Jesus, it was good enough for me.

I had no idea where I was headed, or what would happen once I arrived—if there'd be more names to learn only to have to forget them, more staff to kiss up to, more games to play where odds were, I'd be dealt the losing hand. And though I sat in that waiting room so sweaty that my T-shirt was waterlogged, hanging from me like a sloughing off of my skin, and my lifeless bangs were sticking straight up from my hairline, and my hand was so wet the garbage bag became hard to hold on to, I still managed to rustle up a true sense of relief at never having to return to Redding, to that squat, institutionalized beige house where erasure, disguised as rehabilitation, hijacked the hopes and dreams of so many troubled girls, obliterating them like paper dolls in a hurricane. I was unwilling to be forever lost in the vapid landscape of a psycho-tropic daze.

Hallelujah!

Gwen met me at San Francisco International. As to be expected, there were no exchanges of excitement over being in one another's company. A nod between the two of us stood for what was unspoken. It had been almost seven months since I'd seen her. I sat in the passenger's seat, buckled up, and quickly anchored into the separateness that engulfed us both.

I knew better than to ask questions, because questions required answers, and answers—from me, to Gwen—demanded I have a solid reason for why I "threatened" to poison an entire facility with the very meds meant to poison, I mean, cure me. I would've had to work hard to convince *her*—the same person who'd secretly solicited my father's signature to allow Guideways to administer psychotropic meds to a teenager—that what I *really* needed was to be held, encouraged, and granted the benefit of the doubt.

Was it really my place to tell her that no one should ever be tossed onto a cold, naked floor with no way out, and be threatened that they need to shut down their emotional turmoil on a dime or else suffer more? Why didn't I deserve someone willing to help me through the darkness of the indescribable? It was better that we both stayed quiet.

When the silence broke it was Gwen who made the tear. "You'll be here until I find a placement for you in San Francisco, Regina."

Respite

Jezebel June's house sat in the center of a cul-de-sac near MacDonald Avenue, in a section of Richmond I hadn't known when I lived there with my father. Four and a half years had passed since I was last in the same town where Tom lived. Six months past my sixteenth birthday, which happened without my observing it. It would've been nice to look up my friend from the shelter, Jordy, and Lola was slated to emancipate from Guideways soon, but I'd had no way of reaching either one of them. That was life as a foster child. We were the original rolling stones who gathered no moss.

"You can call me June," the beautiful black woman told me after Gwen's abrupt departure. Her skin, as if the sun had set in honey, was like mine in such a way I'd never seen on anyone other than my mother, Ruby. June had her own glow.

"Don't mind Miss Gwen," she continued, "I've been working with her for a long while now, and every time she drops one of you kids off she says the same thing: "You can address your new foster parent as Ms. June." June mocked Gwen's prim and proper mannerisms. "I'm no 'Ms.,'" she said with a playful edge. We both laughed. I smiled a bit longer than I had in a long while. June promised a sense of good-naturedness I wanted to be around. She was easygoing.

She showed me to my room. But first, we walked up a flight of stairs that had, nailed to the wall on our right, twelve framed images of Jesus in various stages of hardship. I stopped and paid rapt attention to the twelfth picture, the one where Jesus's feet and hands were nailed to the cross he'd been obliged to carry.

"I see you know about the Stations of the Cross?" June asked. I didn't know the images by name, but I figured out the story the pictures told. Something softened in my heart.

"I put these here to remind me to think good on my own mama. Like so many of you kids, us grown people have problems with our people, too. That's why I try and help you, you see. I walk these Stations every day, up and down again. That way I won't forget that there's somebody somewhere who's got it far worse than me, and there ain't a thing I can't overcome."

"Thank you," I told June, and went into my room. I checked beneath the bed, inside the small closet, gauged the distance between the roof and the ground, the front door and my room, the back door. For some reason—unlike Ms. Rosecrans's and that Preacher's houses—June's seemed better suited for Jesus. Something about the way she explained *why* she did things the way she did made sense to me. I allowed myself to give June a chance and at least stay the night.

Sodom & Gomorrah

The next morning was November 18, 1978. The television was so loud it bolted me awake. I got dressed and scuttled downstairs.

What looked like black bodies were scattered and splayed across the screen as if they'd showered down from heaven. People were spread out prone, large arms locked with small arms locked with thick arms and slim ones, laced together like a congregation in silent contemplation, as if in prayer, but they weren't lying there as if in supplication, as if beseeching God for "one more chance." They weren't doing that. They were all dead.

June paced the floor between the kitchen and the living room. The news reported the incident of the Jonestown massacre and I reached for the bag that held my liquid Thorazine. I'd decided I wouldn't give June a hard time about taking it.

"Can you tell me where I can get a spoon?" I asked June. She seemed more jittery than she had the night before.

"Hallelujah!" June shouted out. "The Lord will not be merciful to sinners I say! You see here what happens to sinners?" she asked, pointing at the television screen, her finger jutting back and forth as though she were pushing a button to stop something in a panic, or indicting someone she'd caught in a lie. "The Lord will not be merciful. You cannot, I say, drink from the chalice of the world, and dwell in the house of the Lord. No child in this house can be on drugs. If you on drugs and you're in this house you got's to go."

I was confused.

"Are you sure?" I asked. She placed the palm of her right hand on my forehead and shouted, "Li'l lamb of God, as of now . . . I say as of right now . . . I say . . . as of right here in this minute and by the glory of God . . . you are no longer on them drugs! You are no longer afflicted with the sickness of disobedience! Look what them drugs have done. Them drugs is of them white folks. See what that white man done? He done made believers out of the lost. You ain't no longer lost, you hear me? He drugged them believers with the Kool-Aid of Satan. I say Satan-nananananana. Snake. Give your life over to Christ Jeeeesus!"

June gave me her ultimatum: either drop the meds, or she would drop me someplace else. Gwen had nowhere else to send me. I was not going back into a mental institution–style facility. I dropped Thorazine cold turkey. I spent a day or two vomiting. I had diarrhea. Going up and down those stairs made my head spin. I was frightened to death that the bad part of me, the part that no one wanted, would, again, get the best of me, and ruin this thing I was building with June.

"This here Regina?"

Just like that. Out of nowhere the call came. A man's voice. Deep. Gruff. Talked as if he knew me, firsthand, as if suddenly I was someone who counted.

I continued to live with June, still waited for an opening at some place in San Francisco.

"Yeah, it's me, who's this?" I didn't know any men other than Tom well enough to receive a call from.

"This here Lebanon Johnson. I'm calling on behalf of Ruby Carmichael. You know who that is?"

Ruby? It took a second for memory to catch the name, register it in my mind.

"She with you?" I asked Lebanon Johnson, all the while wondering: *how come Ruby hasn't called?* Why had she put that strange man up to calling her child, who she hadn't seen in at least four years? I couldn't help but wonder if he'd called to tell me my mother had died. June had encouraged me to pray again. I'd prayed a lot as a kid, but lost the strength to do so somewhere between losing Miss Kerr that day in court and waking up in my own excrement one time too many at Guideways. Since arriving at June's, I'd prayed to God to look after my mother. She'd had it real hard. I'd even managed to get a few words in asking him to soften Gwen's heart while he was at it.

Something must be wrong, I thought. The only time I ever heard from anyone from my past was when one of them died. Like that time when I lived with Tom, and Big Mama had called—the only time ever—and told Tom that her daughter Mae Etta had passed from breast cancer. Tom relayed the message to me. I thought about the five kids she'd left behind without fathers to look after them. I thought especially about her daughter Kimberly. I don't remember feeling much of anything else, except I became morbidly afraid of that thing called death.

"C'mon down to the Marina's Edge Motel, room 23, she should be there waiting on you."

Gwen hadn't bothered to enroll me in school. Apparently, Guideways had been held up gathering together any records of my school attendance. Since the local school, John F. Kennedy, would soon be on Christmas break, Gwen thought it better to wait until the New Year to enroll me. Once I gave her my word that I would ask Ruby, or the man she traveled with, for gas money, June agreed to drive me to the hotel to see my mother.

Room 23 had a blue door, a deep-sea-blue-colored door, and was located on the first floor near the ice dispenser. I knocked, and the door creaked open, and there in a black negligee and robe with a built-in black boa that was draped twice around her shoulders stood my mother, Ruby, with a Pall Mall perfectly balanced between her lips, see-through heels, a beehive hairdo, and a fresh set of Lee press-on nails. Red.

"Come on now, Gina, and give your old girl some sugar," Ruby demanded, her standard. She always had a way of talking to me as if we'd just spoken the day before, and not as if years of her being absent should have anything to do with her being there right then.

"Ain't here to talk about the past, now," was her offering for all conversations concerning her whereabouts, and anything else that might compete with the stunningness of her sudden appearance, and perhaps, instead, illuminate her seeming indifference toward parenting. Although I'd later understand how one's shame can easily appear as haughtiness or insignificance. I'm sure in her own way, my mother loved me, no matter how small the amount.

Lebanon, her male companion, looked up when June and I entered. June's auburn hair was pulled away from her face, held in a ponytail. She resembled an even younger version of Ruby. Ruby didn't give her a second look; however, the moment definitely wasn't lost on either June or Lebanon. Glances were exchanged. June decided to wait in the car, and Lebanon, who'd quickly sat up in his chair, paying close attention to our movements, leaned back into a dark corner, next to drawn curtains. He wore dark clothing, most likely black, because I do recall thinking, at the time, how he resembled a black cowboy: Stetson, boots, pants, and all. Black. He stirred ice with a long-handled teaspoon and it clinked up against his caramel-colored glass. A bottle of Bacardi 151 sat in the center of the table.

"I'm here for your court date," Ruby said, to my surprise. Gwen hadn't mentioned anything about my annual custody hearing, to say nothing of my mother visiting, nor had June. Even when I'd told June about Lebanon's call regarding my mother, she'd seemed as surprised as I had.

My . . . mother! I was the poster child of amazement. Not only was I in the presence of the one who'd given birth to me, the one who first set eyes upon me, first held me (I imagined), smelled me, kissed me, and named me, therefore making her my mother, but, also—there I stood, damn near stultified in that motel room, staring at the woman who'd shown up out of nowhere, like a magic trick. Ruby was indeed her own phenomenon. I never felt that I belonged to my mother so much as I did to the astonishment of all the ways she'd lived her life and my very willingness to meet her where she was.

Too afraid to ask questions, too concerned that I would somehow make the dream of my mother! far too real and have it all blow up in my face, I sat, admiringly, at the foot of the king-sized bed and listened, and watched Ruby flit between having Lebanon fill her highball with spirits and filling me in on the happenings of her two sons. How the oldest was doing well in school, and the youngest was still a little bit shy, but "he'll be just fine." Not for one moment did it seem to occur to her that I was not an old friend that needed to be "caught up" with the goings-on of her life, that I was not supposed to be hanging with her in a motel room bordering a feeder road in some shantytown on the wrong side of Richmond.

I wasn't supposed to be sitting there like some lone audience member with a front-row seat to the Ruby Show.

Couldn't she see? I was her youngest daughter, the one she'd let slide past her watch and into the cracks. It was all so fantastic. A spectacle. And I was far too tongue-tied, and all twisted up inside, to know what to do with any of it. I knew that I had to take what she was giving me. However, I wanted, in a bad way, to ask Ruby if she'd come to take me back with her—but then I thought about Miss Kerr, about everything she'd done for me, been to me. I thought about how she'd wanted what was best for me. Fought for me. Something in me had changed. I'd realized that although it was natural for me to call for Ruby in sadness or distress, when it came down to it, she never asked me about *me*, never really did much in the way of what I needed, or wanted, never told me what I needed to hear. I would learn, later in life, that my assessment of that moment was accurate, and that my mother, like so many survivors of harrowing experiences, didn't know how to work through her own devastation to show up, be there for the one who needed her most, me.

I left room 23 with the blue door $100 richer. Ruby had sneaked it into my palm as I was leaving. "Hey, wait a sec, Gina-girl," she'd said, laying her hand of the same color as mine on mine, and, with a sleight of hand, transferring the folded bill to me.

"They ain't feeding my baby right," she said. "You look hungry as hell." She laughed her kind of laugh, that full-body thing that seemed to stop time in its tracks and enchantingly expunge all the loss that had accumulated, binding us.

I hadn't prayed for a $100 bill, but I was happy to receive it. I didn't want to break it, I wanted to save it, smooth out its edges, and smell it for traces of my mother's hand, her purse, the places she'd been. Anything reminiscent of her. After I paid June, I made an intention to save the rest so that, one day, I'd buy something to remind me of my mama. I believed that God had answered one prayer: I was happy to see that my mother, my Ruby, was still alive, crazy, and still her wild and not-to-be-controlled-by-anyone self.

Book Three

January

1979. A placement became available in San Francisco. Gwen moved me in on a weekday when the current residents were in school. Her thinking was that it would be less disruptive to the already established vibe the girls had going on and it would give me a chance to meet the two black women she'd successfully convinced to become my "last hope."

Upon arrival at the George Walker Group Home for Girls, I met Barbara Nelson. Barbara wore a beige cashmere sweater over a crisp white shirt with a popped-up collar. She was so En Vogue.

"I like your shoes," was the first thing I said, suddenly remembering Lola's advice about Morris. Or maybe June's praying had taken effect and I was softening.

"These old things," said Barbara. Those "old things" just so happened to be a pair of driving moccasins by Gucci. She had the most perfect Afro I had ever seen, as if she'd stood in the mirror all day patting it into shape with a silk scarf, like my mother, Ruby, had made it a habit to do. Barbara looked like a perfect collision between Native American and African American bloodlines, with features very much like Diana Ross: a mountain-peak-sharp nose, cheekbones like rising moons beneath her midnight-black hair.

"Do you have your hair done weekly?" Barbara asked. She spoke as if she were trying to keep marbles from falling from her mouth. I lied and answered, "I sure do," because I wanted the new Jheri-curl hairstyle that made black girls who needed it look like we had good hair. I needed it.

We lived in an Eichler house in Diamond Heights, and ours was the only house on the block with a bright red door and a shiny brass door knocker. A tree grew from the middle of an open-air atrium, and we walked, every day, across thick-piled white shag carpet through the house's two sunken living rooms. We had plenty of Price Club food to eat. We sat at a dinner table, even if only to stare at one another, or the food—Barbara demanded we do so because it was important we learn the ways of civility. We had strikes against us, we girls. We were black; there was a Mexican girl here or there who came and went, but it was us black girls she was most concerned about. We were the ones who had the uphill battle to overcome our circumstances. We each slept on an expensive bed, complete with frame, headboard, comforter, and 100 percent percale sheets by Marimekko. Although Barbara never said that just because we were black it didn't mean we shouldn't aspire toward the finer things in life, it became evident in her actions, in what she valued. There were six of us girls at the time of my arrival and we were all shades of black. It was the first time in a while my outside matched my insides in terms of the quality of my living environment. I took that to mean that Ms. Barbara cared about us girls.

The residents at GW loved to sit and share their war stories about how they ended up in foster care. I never wanted to tell anyone my business. I'd lived that madness once and wasn't about to hash it up again and again. I wanted to get as far away from tragedy as possible. It was hard enough hearing them talk. While the other girls chased men, dope, and empty dreams, I picked up the dictionary for the first time in a long while, and read it at my leisure. I didn't tell anyone about the Preacher's son visiting my room every night the entire time I stayed in that house. Or the year and a half I lost in a drug-induced daze at Guideways. I acted as if I were still at June's with the Stations of the Cross keeping watch over me. June had taught me a prayer I had enjoyed learning and I prayed it each night before falling to sleep:

Our Father, Who art in Heaven,
hallowed be thy name. Thy Kingdom come, thy will be done
on earth as it is in Heaven. Give us this day our daily bread,
and forgive us our trespasses, as we forgive those who trespass against us.
And lead us not into temptation, but deliver us from evil.
For thine is the Kingdom and the glory.
Amen.

Someone has led this child to believe

The butter-colored folder with "Regina Louise" hand-printed on the tab lay on the desk in the small office where the house parents slept. It seemed a contradiction to call the hired help house parents. They were paid $5 an hour to meet the state-required ordinance of having us, as property of the state, supervised. Honestly, I would've preferred Barbara or her mother's caretaking. They had good intentions, those two.

The lady on duty, Ms. Jardinière, a Geechee-speaking woman from South Carolina, busied herself with doing laundry. She was one to sit out in the atrium, dip snuff, and spit it out to the tune of the dryer cycle as the clothes and sneakers tumbled and thumped their way to dry. If the dryer beat the washer, she'd switch to chewing on ice chips or rocks of powdered starch to bide her time while folding sheets, linens, towels. I knew I had time to read the entire file if I wanted. I didn't waste any of it.

This file wasn't as thick as the one I'd found at Guideways. Most of the contents were on official pleading papers, and there were a few letters. I read the most recent one from Guideways.

Guideways Treatment Center

████████████

Redding California
96099

████████████

November 21, 1978

Dear Ms. Forde:

It is with restrained relief that I write this letter to you, informing
you of our unanimous decision to terminate Regina from our
program. From the moment she arrived at Guideways, Regina
became a resident who needed far more interaction than any other
resident in our care. She has exhausted our staff.

Her frequent violations of the rules; touching other residents without
permission, using the telephone, swimming without permission
which nearly resulted in her drowning (as you know we had to rush
her to Mercy hospital by ambulance.)

I was made aware—in the middle of the night—that Regina had
attempted to poison the residents and staff with the incident
involving her meds, and the milk container that had to be replaced.

It is only because Regina confessed to the infraction that we, the
agency, did not file charges.

Regina is the most self-destructive child this agency has ever dealt
with.

Regards,

████████████, MA, LCSW

I read a short note that had been written to Barbara Nelson about me, encouraging her to take me in.

Barbara,

I'm writing again to see if you have an opening for my client. I believe that you and your mother are the only ones who might get it through to her that she has an identity crisis, that she is a black girl in need of guidance from her own people. I don't believe that it will be an easy thing to do; I do think, however, that George Walker will be a good fit for Regina.

Between you and me, I think someone has led this child to believe she is above-average intelligence when she is marginal at best. When I last asked Regina what she planned to do with her life after the age of majority, she told me she's planning to attend college. I believe that Regina thinks she can climb any mountain or hurdle without preparation. This is delusional, but on second thought, with her vindictive and manipulative ways this child just might succeed.

Because Regina is considered high risk the county will reimburse at the highest BHI rate.

Thank you,

████████ MSW, II

Marginal

All the girls at GW attended an outside school, which meant I'd have to as well. Barbara was all about raising the field of opportunity for the "young ladies" in her care. On that first day, she told me that since I was closer to eighteen than I wasn't, I was old enough to sign myself up for school. Barbara handed me a packet and instructed me to hand it off to the counselor they were sure to assign me. I left with the other residents and walked through Diamond Heights canyon to school.

As Barbara had said, I was assigned a counselor and turned over the envelope. I wanted to be in school. I needed access to library books, to people who might be able to help me become better than I was. After what I'd read in that file, it was clear I must be a psychopathic monster. I had to fix that. I wouldn't stop until I did.

After all the proficiency exams were administered, taken, and scored, it was decided that except for math, I was functioning, academically, at grade level for my age: I was, officially, a twelfth grader.

I met "Harry the Hippie" my first week at McAteer High. He was a middle-aged Shaun Cassidy, long hair and all. He wore a green army jacket and jeans and strolled through our campus motored by his smile. Harry taught an advanced psychology class to students who had tested high in verbal communication and empathy skills. Since I was the new girl, everyone was interested in learning something about me.

"Come on, tell us your name, something about yourself, and where you're transferring from," Harry asked, in rapid fire. I didn't think about what came next.

"My name is Regina, I'm seventeen, and I turn eighteen in May. The last placement, before the one I now live in, George Walker Group Home for Girls, was called Guideways. I was terminated for standing up for what I believed was wrong." I felt so completely self-assured. My having my say wasn't so much about needing to be right as it was about possessing a deep need to let people know what was happening to kids like me.

After class, Harry caught up to me and told me how "bitchin'" it was that I could just share what I had without blinking. He said that he imagined I hadn't had a chance to apply for colleges, given what I had said. I told him how right he was, and that I'd imagined I could go to college, but had no idea how to get there.

"We'll figure something out," he said.

"Do you know what *marginal* means?" I asked Harry. He asked why and I told him about what I'd read in the file.

"Oh, yeah?" he asked, his face painted in disbelief. "Well, you can tell whoever told you that, that I said to give you a chance to speak your mind, and you'll be sure to blow theirs." That's all I needed to hear.

From that moment on, I spent every spare minute educating myself on how to become as normal as everyone around me and to better blend in to the crowd of kids who had expectations of doing something great beyond high school. Whatever that meant. The GW house had bookshelves stuffed to capacity. I took the dictionary I was reading everywhere I went, along with books about Dick Gregory, Stokely Carmichael, and Maya Angelou. My carrying the dictionary wasn't merely about looking up every word I encountered, but more so a chance to keep Miss Kerr alive in my mind.

I looked up "marginal" in the dictionary. What meaning I could understand at the time had to do with a margin as the "edge" of something. I pulled out a piece of ruled paper and studied the red line demarcating the left edge. In the margin, I wrote: *This is not me.* And that is when it occurred to me what Gwen meant. Even though I aspired to become anything I wanted, as Miss Kerr had encouraged, from Gwen's perspective I would never make it to the center because I was destined to be trapped within the small and ill-defined borders of the margins. If that's what she thought about me, she had another thing coming.

Above average

At McAteer, I finally found a place where I fit right in, no explanations, no apologies; I was just a regular girl doing regular-girl things. I got myself voted president of the choir. The vote was unanimous. I selected the music we sang, the types of events we participated in, and I assisted in preparing the choir to sing in school talent shows, both regionally and nationally.

I even accepted three invitations to the same senior prom, but eventually I had to assist the two guys I ultimately said no to in finding suitable dates. This was easy enough because I'd made friends with many of the choir girls, and two of them, Monique and Angela, were available as dates and accepted.

To pay for my prom gown, shoes, stockings, jewelry, and hairdo, I needed money. As a resident, I earned $5 a week to maintain my room and complete my chores, which included cleaning my room, changing bed linens, keeping clothes hung up, and cleaning a bathroom or two. Sometimes we'd have to help Ms. Jardinière or one of the other house parents set and clear the table for dinner.

So, I took on a paper route. Each morning before any of the other people in the house awoke, I'd hop on the bike I'd borrowed from the next-door neighbor and pedal up to where Amber Drive became Duncan Street, cross Diamond Heights Boulevard, and pick up my bundle of papers. I'd take the time to fold and rubber band each paper, stick them all in my bib, and hustle up and down those hills that made up the surrounding Eichler housing communities. I was a beautiful date in my baby-blue asymmetric-hem dress and silver high-heeled shoes. So many times, I'd watched as my Ruby slathered herself in bold-colored eye shadows and lush eyelashes, in shimmering materials and panty hose with seams that ran the length of the backs of her long legs. Secretly I'd keep an eye on her beauty rituals from behind a crack in the door and I'm lucky I did, because when it was my turn, I knew what I wanted, and liked the way I did it. That prom, and the ones after that, ushered me into the undiscovered world of my own girl-self.

By the time I turned eighteen, and everyone in my class had started all that talk about our pending graduation day and what to do regarding *Grad Nite '80*, and what we were all going to do after we finished high school, someone in the downtown school-district office had realized that while I may've had the scholastic aptitude to be a senior in high school, I lacked nearly four years' worth of the state-required credits necessary to graduate.

"What would you like to do?" my counselor, Freidna Howell, asked. The question itself was as foreign to me as it was to be standing in her office in the first place. I didn't know I had options.

This could mean that I'd have to leave the George Walker group home—even if I had nowhere to go.

Stay

Gwen and Barbara agreed that it would be in my best interest to stay another year at GW, that I could use the extra time to finish high school and come up with a plan as to what I would do upon graduation, which automatically triggered my emancipation from the system. Both women made it clear to me that what I was asking was unprecedented.

"I think I can get into a college," I said. "My psychology teacher thinks I might be able to get into Antioch University or University of California, Santa Cruz." I told her how Harry felt that Santa Cruz would be best suited for me, given they had more of an experiential approach and allowed students to present their exams orally.

While Gwen wasn't necessarily convinced that I would get into *any* type of college, she was willing to at least work on getting me the extra time. I never let on that I was aware of her low expectations of me. Anyway, something in me felt sorry for what she would look like if I told her I knew. I just couldn't bring myself to do it. Instead. I made a vow to prove her wrong.

"Summertime"

"You could become an opera singer, you know," said Mr. Meggars, my music teacher. "Bet you'd sound great singing 'Summertime.'"

"What's that?" I asked. Mr. Meggars, along with Harry and Mrs. Goldberg—the dance teacher—was one of my favorite teachers.

"Repeat after me," he said, using two fingers to pound A minor. It was odd sounding, that key. I was afraid of it, afraid I'd sound too much like a white person. I didn't know any black folks who sounded like they were holding in their rectum while simultaneously pushing out a screeching sound.

"I can't do that," I said.

"Why not?" Mr. Meggars asked.

"I'll get laughed at."

"Jessye Norman doesn't care if people laugh at her. Neither does Leontyne Price. You've heard the story of Marian Anderson, right?"

"Who?"

"What about *Pippin*, or *Porgy and Bess*?" Now he really had my interest.

"What about *Porgy and Bess*?" I asked, and he told me, and I shared my story with him.

I decided to give it one more try. He tapped the key and I repeated after him. I agreed to meet him in the choir room during lunch period. Repeatedly, I sang the words behind Mr. Meggars's lead, until I had that song tattooed in my cells. I'd admitted I couldn't practice at home. The girls I lived with came from "East Paly-Alto," the Sunnydale projects, and the notorious "Pink Palace" public housing in San Francisco. They were tough. They weren't about to let me blast out opera, no matter if famous black women had worked like dogs to make it so they could sing it professionally, onstage, in public.

One girl, Alisha, told me straight up: "I ain't to be more than my mama, and 'cause bus drivin' is good by her, it's good by me." I wanted to be so much more than both her mother and my own. I was all I had. I was dually confused and fascinated by the circumference of limit she'd already drawn around her life. Drawn to Alisha in a sisterly way, I wanted to give her a piece of my desire for more. I'd hoped that Barbara's ways of living the good life would rub off on Alisha. But mostly, Barbara was seen by the residents as a white woman in black women's clothing. Bougie. A sellout. Not black enough.

Therefore, albeit heartbroken, I was not surprised some twenty years later when I—as a volunteer singer in the Glide Memorial Choir—crossed paths with Alisha. I'd unknowingly adopted her family to give Christmas presents to. Strangely enough, my intuition guided me to shop for the family of seven as though they were my own. I'd raised enough money from fund-raising from my salon clients to purchase three times the amount they requested. A red bicycle for the smallest boy, Nintendo for the eldest. As I searched the pews, on gift-giving day, that were alphabetized, I kept passing a woman who looked vaguely familiar. I called out "Alisha Walker," repeatedly until that woman called me by my name, "Regina, is that you?" I was bewildered as the young girl I once knew stood in front of me as the fate I was fiercely determined to have nothing to do with.

Mr. Meggars handed me the application for the California Music Educators Association (CMEA) music festival. He had nominated me to sing in the opera category. He thought I might have a chance to be seen and heard by a college scout or something. He put in the effort by researching the opportunities, and gave me all the space I needed, not just to learn, but to improve.

On the day of my solo performance, I wore a red-and-white pinstriped linen pantsuit that I'd borrowed from Barbara. The more I helped myself, the more Barbara came around to liking and supporting me. I attributed that to the shift in reputation the girls were making for themselves. People began to see that not *everyone* at the GW home was considered a "toss-up," a girl who'd let boys have her any way they wanted during lunchtime, like a tossed salad. It seemed that everyone knew we didn't have *real* parents looking out for us, so we were easy targets. Another thing I wasn't was a "hose monster," a girl who would give a guy a blow job on demand, as some of the girls were called as they walked down the halls of McAteer. That was the first time I'd ever heard of such a thing. I thought it repulsive and couldn't imagine why anyone would want to do such a thing. I let the girls know that I didn't think it was a good idea to do things that would ruin their reputations. Soon enough, word got around that a few of the girls were turning over a new leaf.

So, I stood there in the soundproof studio, behind layers of thick glass, and switched the microphone on. I took Mr. Meggars's advice and let the mournfulness of want roll off my tongue as if I were that little baby I sang to, as if my "mommy and daddy" were standing by, as if it were all right that they weren't. Ms. Barbara and Mr. Meggars were waiting once I'd finished.

First prize was a Command Performance. I received the next category down, a Standing Ovation, and I was good with that, because in less than a year I'd gone from clawing at the walls and screaming into the slit of light in the SHU box to receiving a standing ovation for something I was brave enough to hold on to until the right moment, when my song, my soul, had a chance to be seen and heard.

Diagnostic and Statistical Manual
of Mental Disorders

I took a trip to the San Francisco Public Library and found my way to the reference librarian and checked out a copy of the *Diagnostic and Statistical Manual of Mental Disorders*, 2nd edition (DSM-II). I made it my business to find out everything I could about some of the words Gwen used to describe me in that letter to Barbara: *delusional, identity crisis, manipulative, vindictive.*

Deep down, I was searching for a better understanding of what had happened to me, what was wrong with me, and what I could do to be different in a way that would stick, that would show the adults in my life—Gwen, Barbara, and even Ruby or Big Mama or Lula Mae should they ever want to know anything about me—that I could become what I wanted to become. I wanted to be the first person from Barbara's group home to graduate high school—not just take the GED because I wasn't considered smart enough, or disciplined, or willing to do whatever it took to close the gap on my own disadvantages, but to earn a high school diploma on my own merit. To say that I did it! And have a chance to attend the college of *my* choice.

I did not find what I was looking for in that manual that day. I did, however, read about psychosis, given I had been diagnosed as psychotic at Guideways, and the characteristics of the mental disorder: delusions, distortions of reality, and hallucinations weren't behaviors I exhibited; rather, they had been side effects of the medications I was administered. If anything, I would consider my "condition" this: I had an adverse reaction to my childhood, to being unwanted, rejected, and pathologized for it. There was nothing for me to be loyal to other than my own recklessness, truancy, and the fact that no matter how hard I wanted to belong to something, *to someone*, I was stuck in a system hell-bent on marginalizing my potential to want more and do more.

Most likely to become mayor of San Francisco

"Regina Louise," announced Father John Lo Schiavo, the president of the University of San Francisco. As I walked across the stage in the USF gymnasium, my hair was coiffed in soft ringlet curls, I sported faux-alligator five-inch heels, and I had on a tan dress with delicate magenta cherry blossoms beneath my black-and-gold graduation gown.

Barbara's daughter was also graduating that day from University High School, an exclusive private school in Pacific Heights, and therefore Barbara was unable to participate on my behalf. Neither was Gwen Forde able to attend. Sure, it was just cause to be sad or disappointed, but I sidestepped those emotions and assured myself that one day I'd graduate from college and the people I wanted to be there, would be. In my wanting to get out of the group home without one incident report, I took it well when I asked Barbara if I could invite Miss Kerr and was told no. I wasn't surprised. Barbara bought me my class ring to show how proud she was of me. She'd given it to me earlier.

My choir buddies Holly, Martin, Colleen, and Jim, and I each took a turn singing our solo parts of the song I'd suggested for our graduation: "I Sing the Body Electric," from the hit film *Fame*. By song's end, the entire gym, all 800-plus people, was on its feet.

After the ceremony, I heard a familiar voice behind me say, "Why come you didn't call me and tell me they voted my baby most likely to be the damn mayor of San Francisco?" I turned, and there stood Ruby in a purple dress. Simple. Her hair was straightened and styled in a shoulder-length bob.

Ruby surprised me when she handed me my yearbook, which I thought my friends had taken up a collection to buy me. But somehow—and Ruby wouldn't let on how—there she was, standing there with it. Like a magic trick. A phenomenon. Spectacular.

Later, in her hotel room Ruby let me know that Barbara had tracked her down and insisted that she bear witness to something so many doubted would *ever* happen, including her. Barbara had paid for everything.

One week after graduation, bearing a footlocker that contained a bottle of wine, a wine opener, a steam iron, and a fox-fur coat—all compliments of Barbara—and carrying whatever didn't fit in the locker in yet another garbage bag, I walked out of the GW group home and into a cab headed to a friend's house. I'd received eight offer letters, one from each of the schools I'd applied to, through the various universities' Equal Opportunity Programs, without which I would not have been able to attend college. Occidental College. Chico State. California College of the Arts. Antioch. University of San Francisco. San Francisco State. City College of San Francisco. Mills College.

The Child

September 8, 1979   Date of Hearing: September 18, 1979

REGINA LOUISE–#49990-(16)-   Born: May 2, 1962, Austin Texas

Family:
Father: Tom Brock (37)   ████████████████████
Mother: Ruby Carmichael   Texas, exact whereabouts?
Stepmom: Nadine Hathaway   ████████████████████
Half-sibs: female 6½   With parents
Female 4½   With parents

CHILD'S LEGAL RESIDENCE:
The minor's residence was established in ████████████████
in 1976 by her father's residence. The minor's mother has legal
residence in Texas.

WHEREABOUTS OF MINOR:
The minor is in the George Walker Group Home, ████████████████
████████████. She was placed there January 11, 1979.

COUNSEL: None.

REASON FOR HEARING: Annual review

JURISDICTIONAL RECOMMENDATION:
Continue dependency under section 300a of the W & I code.

PRIOR DEPENDENCY RECORD:
6/25/76 ████████ Adjudged dependent child, placement ordered.
The last hearing was May 12, 1978.

FAMILY FUNCTIONING:

Mr. Brock continues to reside in ████████████████ with his family. He has not initiated contact with Regina or this worker during the past year. Regina initiates all contacts, which are very minimal and infrequent. Regina continues to try and engage him in some kind of parent-child relationship. Mr. Brock has been unwilling to be involved in any planning for Regina and has begun to deny paternity to this worker.

Mrs. Carmichael, too, has made no inquiries regarding Regina's welfare that this worker is aware of. From time to time, she calls the staff and promises to call Regina and according to the group home, it upsets Regina when mother doesn't follow through. Apparently, Mrs. Carmichael has made several promises to send money or other gifts but has not followed through. Mrs. Carmichael has been separated from Regina for many years prior to 1976. She indicated that she was very young when Regina was born and she was unable, for a variety of reasons, to accept responsibility for her daughter. Mrs. Carmichael indicated that she has been a good mother to two young sons born when she was more mature and able to take on parenting responsibilities. She stated that she cannot undo the injustice that she has done to Regina but she would like to be her friend and to provide support and guidance where possible. Mrs. Carmichael talked with my supervisor, ████████████████, and indicated that she would contact this writer later regarding Regina's custody but to date no further contact has been made.

THE CHILD:

Regina's problem continues to be one of having to live somewhere. For all practical purposes, she has been abandoned by both parents. Regina, 18, is an attractive, articulate, and an extremely narcissistic and vindictive young woman.

Regina's personal needs always seem to take precedence and if things do not work out according to her plan, she creates situations to cause total confusion and chaos. This was particularly true as she approached high school graduation. Regina was able to show signs of maturity; however, it seems obvious that graduation was as much a frightening experience as it was to anticipate.

Upon meeting Regina for the first time, one is impressed with a seemingly sophisticated, mature young woman. However, after a limited amount of contact, it becomes obvious that she is very immature and lacking in self-confidence. Impulse control has improved but not to the extent that she could function independently.

Regina has natural leadership qualities but is unable to handle this positive aspect of her personality. Recently Regina was terminated from her last placement for behavior problems. ██████████ the director at Guideways, stated that Regina was the most difficult girl they had ever had. Regina is described as charming, bright, and totally destructive to any kind of organized program.

At this point in time, the goals for Regina include graduation from high school and preparation to emancipate. Whether or not either or both of these goals can be met in the next year is questionable. She has missed a great deal of school and she has not attended public school in approximately three years. She needs to develop social skills, which will help her to get through school successfully and also help her to cope with society in general. Regina tends to deal with people very superficially or she tunes them out completely.

The progress report dated October 2, 1978 from Guideways stated that, "At times Regina is extremely uncooperative in every aspect: disobeys house rules, defiant, rebellious, rude to the girls and staff. Conversely, Regina has the capacity of being quiet, friendly, cooperative, polite, and respectful to everyone in the house." Regina attempted to poison the entire Guideways facility on November 17, 1979, which was the action that finally resulted in her permanent termination.

EVALUATION:
Regina seems to have found her niche at the George Walker Group Home. She met her match in terms of two strong-willed black women (director and house parent) who were not impressed with her "cutesy" little-girl antics and have forced her to accept responsibility for her own behavior.

WORKERS PLAN:
Regina is a very needy person and tends to make demands seemingly to test out whether or not support is "for real." Realistically speaking, she will probably leave the program when she graduates, but it is doubtful that she will be emotionally secure enough to handle her life.

I will close case upon her graduation from high school.

FREQUENCY OF VISITS:

Monthly-regular consultations with group home staff.

RECOMMENDATION:

Jurisdictional:
1. Continue as 300a

Dispositional:
2. Continue as dependent child

3. Continue 361(B).

4. Continue committed to social service placement

5. Children's Shelter or Emergency Foster Home placement or replacement.

6. ███████████████████████; parents to reimburse.

7. Social Services to authorize medical, dental remedial care.

8. Social Services authorized to temporarily return minor home.

9. Review Date: February 12, 1980

Respectfully submitted,

████████████████

Social Casework Specialist II

████████████████ Social Service Department

Read and considered by:

████████████████

Take care of my girl now

August 27, 1981. The Desoto taxi pulled up to the curb in front of 800 Font Boulevard. I stepped out and stood for a moment, wanting to take it all in. There I was, in front of my dorm—Mary Ward Hall. Nobody back home in Texas would have believed it, even if they were standing right there beside me. No girl from any of the group homes I'd lived in would have believed it, either. But there I was, stuffed to the seams with hope, joy, fear, and excitement, again in the middle of a dream of my own making. I was far too overwhelmed by it all at the time to fully understand the value of making myself feel so pleased. I had made a plan, a solemn vow, and I'd stuck to it. I'd had a choice, a say, a chance to do something with my own life. And there I was, in the proof of it.

I'd planned to arrive before the dorms were flooded by families dropping off their kids. I didn't want to be seen exiting a cab, or telecast that I was alone. But from the looks of the crowds all around, it quickly became obvious that many other people had the same idea. Though it was two hours before the official registration time, I saw girls following behind mothers while fathers and younger siblings carried luggage, pillows, stuffed animals. I grabbed my footlocker and garbage bag and walked toward the crowds that were starting to build at the registration tables on the lawn in front of Mary Ward Hall. It was hard to believe: I was here. I . . . was . . . here!

No one else who'd been through GW had ever graduated and gone on to attend college. Many of those other girls plotted out ways to get pregnant, so that they could be placed in unwed mothers' homes. Far too many were "strongly" encouraged to join the military. There, they would be sure to get three square meals a day, clothing, and shelter. And medical coverage. The military would be an alternative to having nothing.

I didn't have anyone to tell me what to look forward to regarding campus life. But I was tired of strangers telling me what to do. I wanted to make friends, see the world through the eyes of possibility. Here was my chance to learn to do life my way, whatever that turned out to be. I was scared, a little bit sad that I was alone, but also overjoyed that I'd kept my word, didn't lose sight, and did what I said I would.

My roommate, Tracy Richman, had already picked her side of the double closet–sized room by the time I'd checked in, picked up my information packet and keys (the first time in my life I'd ever had a set of keys to anything), and trudged my things up the elevator and to our room. She was pretty, petite, and Jewish. She wore her tightly coiled hair in an asymmetrical bob and sported high-top Reeboks and a pair of light blue distressed Guess jeans with three-inch zippers on the hemline. My mouth watered. Her nails were long, oval, and perfectly manicured. Barbara and her daughter would often go and have their nails and toes done, so I knew a little something about that. But those jeans were a must-have.

"Oh my God, you must be my new roomie!?" Tracy stated more than asked. I was relieved that she didn't seem too surprised that I was alone. She, her father, and her best friend, Marnie, had flown in that morning from Sherman Oaks, the pinnacle of all things Valley. And Tracy was a genuine Valley Girl before the term made its way into popular culture.

Her father, Neil, moved in and out of our tiny room dropping off suitcase after suitcase on Tracy's side of the room, which quickly threatened to overtake mine, and Tracy did not hesitate to boss Neil around. She told Neil where to place things, how to place them, and to "Hurry. Go! Get the rest." One part of me thought her completely disrespectful—the people I came from, like Ruby, Tom, and the Cavanaughs, would never have stood for that. But another part of me recognized it straightaway, because Barbara allowed her daughter to speak to her with the same sassiness Tracy displayed. Many times, it'd been difficult to keep my mouth shut and not tell Barbara's daughter, Mary, to "take it easy, that's your mother. You have no idea how lucky you are to have one. How I'd kill to have one of my own." But that was none of my business, just like it was none of mine to say anything to Tracy.

I'd be a liar if I didn't admit that I was desperate to know what it felt like to belong to somebody in the kind of way where one could mouth off that way without consequences. I kind of believed that's what families were for: to show folks how to stand their ground, to learn to ask for what they wanted, to allow people to push them around until they could learn to stand up for themselves. Family, I imagined, was what shaped people into who they became.

There was no time for me to feel sorry for myself about what I didn't have, although my roommate's situation provided ample opportunity: Neil and Marnie helped her decorate her side of the room, and then her father gave her a credit card for any incidentals that showed up, and told her he'd see her at Thanksgiving. And just before Neil left he turned to me and asked, "You know any good nail salons?" Confused, I answered yes without thinking about it. Neil smiled and held his hand out and said, "Gimme five." I slapped his hand, smiled awkwardly, and thought that was the end of it. But it wasn't.

"You take good care of my girl, now!" Neil called to me over his shoulder.

Ordinary People

I settled into school as well as could be expected. Made a few friends. Like most freshmen, I tried getting through the general-education requirements first, before I could get to the business of deciding on a major. I took electives in human sexuality, theater, social psychology, and ethnic studies. I signed up to be a teacher's assistant for my anthropology professor. I was fascinated by how much there was to learn about people by observing their cultural practices.

My professor thought I was unusual—"exotic," he said—and told me he'd love for me to join him and his wife in a swingers' event. I asked around about swingers, what they did, what kind of people I could expect to be there. I probably don't need to state the obvious, that I squashed that invite and withdrew from the class. I wanted to try new things, but not with a sixty-something guy who resembled a boney and aged Jerry Garcia. Even still, he gave me my first A-plus, and I say "gave" because I'm not sure how I earned it given that I had stopped attending the class weeks before it ended. There was so much to learn, least of which included sharing sex partners with salacious old men.

I wanted to hear what everyone had to say, I wanted to be everything all at once. I noticed that many, if not all, of the girls I hung out with had interesting opinions about politics and religion, and knew the party for which their parents voted. I didn't really know what they were talking about when it came to "Democrats" and "Republicans."

"Hey Genie," said Robyn, a new friend, a Jewish girl from Laguna Beach. I let her call me "Genie" because I heard Miss Kerr's name in it:

Jeannie. "How do your parents vote? I imagine they vote blue given that you guys are black?"

"Yep," I lied. "How did you know that?" I was dead serious.

"Duh . . ." Robyn teased, as if I should have known.

In fact, I had no idea how any adult I'd ever met voted. I was a lifetime, at the very least, behind what those kids knew, unable to keep up when conversations veered toward class or race. I didn't really know anything about President Ronald Reagan and to tell the truth, I soon learned I didn't really care. If politics couldn't hold me, or feed me, I didn't have the time to discuss it as though doing so were a matter of life and death. My politics were self-proclaimed and my best bet was to do whatever it took to remain positive and hopeful.

I received invitations to mother-daughter teas from various sororities, both black and white, but politely refused to attend always claiming to be overbooked with studying. Father-daughter dances were also out of the question. I didn't want to explain to anyone why I never spoke about family, received no phone calls, letters, or birthday cards, and had no care packages to get me through finals. I began to send those things to myself. I bought myself birthday cards, small gifts, and treats. When I received As or Bs on my report cards, I'd walk over to Stonestown Galleria and treat myself to a Baskin-Robbins sundae. My favorite was the Banana Royale. I'd ask for extra nuts on the bottom, layered with hot butterscotch, bananas, and two scoops of Quarterback Crunch. And of course, I had it with whipped cream. Cherry on top. I loved eating that sundae down to the very last bite.

I wrote letters addressed to myself, "signed" by whichever adult I decided had written to me. I made up names like Aunt Sophia or Grandma Myrtle. I mostly put on the show for roommates or close friends. Once I sent myself a $20 bill from Miss Kerr, for a "job well done" when I aced a sociology quiz. I used that for two trips to Baskin-Robbins. I enjoyed it almost as much as if she'd sent the gift to me herself. My philosophy was to use my imagination to see things the way I thought they should be, and maybe one day could be, and work to no end to make things happen.

It was a Friday night, and the main campus had cleared out by the time classes had let out. There was nothing really happening in the dorms, so I asked Tracy if she'd like to join me and see the movie *Ordinary People*. Neither of us had heard of it, but it starred Mary Tyler Moore. I knew her as That Girl and she was funny as hell. What could go wrong with that?

A lot.

By the time Timothy Hutton had witnessed his brother's body get swallowed by the ocean, then slit his wrist, and then admit that he was aware that his mother hated him, I was done in. The heaviness of the film, especially the brutal disregard that Mary Tyler Moore's character showed for Timothy Hutton's character, was enough to make me want to slit my own wrist. I left the theater barely able to speak. All the way back to my room I felt as if I were choking on my own trauma. Tracy and I didn't exchange one word. All the way back I wanted to scream, cry, hide, kill something, blame someone. I took a shower, and it was there I broke down. I scrubbed my body and cried. No, I wailed into my soapy rag. There was no one I could call and ask what the feeling was, why it felt as though I suddenly had the Empire State Building on my shoulders, coming out my stomach. I felt as if someone or something close to me had died, and maybe something had; maybe what I experienced that night was a glimpse into the deadweight I carried, the burden of my own ambiguous loss and what I'd come to know many years later as disenfranchised grief, a condition that comes about because a survivor feels as though her grief is unmerited. Timothy Hutton's mother hated him. She didn't want him. My mother didn't want me, which translated to she hated me, that Miss Kerr and Gwen and Ms. Barbara hated me, that Big Mama and Edith hated me, that anyone I'd ever met and didn't want me hated me. It was more awareness than I could manage. I was most afraid though, that maybe I hated me.

That night I made a solemn vow to become a social worker. I was going to change the system, find a way to help kids, each one at a time, if that's what it took, no matter how difficult.

A few days later, after I regained a bit of perspective and armed myself with some righteous indignation, I marched right on over to the J. Paul Leonard Library. I approached the librarian and asked, "Can you show me where I can find a book, or a few books, on how to live in the world after emancipating from the foster-care system?" The librarian gave me a look.

"What class is this for?" she asked. I told her it wasn't for a class, but that it was for me; I needed help understanding what it meant to have gone through the system, and I needed to know if there were any books that could guide me on things like how to be an adult, save money, and understand why I became so sad about a movie. She listened, bewildered.

"Here," she said, and scribbled a line of letters and numbers onto a slip of paper. She directed me to another woman, a volunteer, who was eager to help me find the book, which wasn't what I was looking for. The title was something like *Status and Transitions of Youth in Board and Care Institutions*. It was more of a highly technical report of why, and how, kids entered institutions, but didn't deal at all with how to manage one's life after emancipation.

That day, I made a second vow: I swore to God that one day I'd write the book I wanted to read, a book that would be there for the young girl or boy who wanted to know how to make sense of the great big world they'd been literally dropped into like a solitary sock in a giant spin cycle; a world where they wouldn't need to rely on lying in order to feel like they fit in. I vowed to make a way where there wasn't one. After all, I'd learned in my black studies class that this was what we black people always did. We were known for always coming back for our own: this one cared for that one, and we played the act of kinship forward like nobody's business. I wanted other black children lost in foster care to be more than just ordinary; I wanted every one of us to know what it felt like, sounded like, looked like to be extraordinary.

Closeted holiday

Since I'd entered college through the Equal Opportunity Program, everything, including housing, food, medical expenses, books, and supplies, was included in the financial aid package I'd been awarded. I took the fact that I'd been "awarded" all that money to mean that I'd done something great to receive it. It was, again, a time that I felt my insides matched up to what was happening in the outside world. My first couple of years, I dove into my studies with zeal. The way I saw it was, if the folks behind the awarding needed me to perform for them by keeping my grades at an above-average level, well, I aimed to please. I needed somebody to expect something from me, push me once I tired of pushing myself. In the beginning of my time as a student, I rarely lost faith in going for what I wanted; I hit it hard, and was always open to how to hit it even harder. But no matter how hard I worked, the feeling of not being good enough was pervasive. I felt it in the way people looked at me whenever I tried to answer questions regarding my family of origin or lack thereof. I'd play it off as if everything was *just fine* the way it was.

My first semester was nearing its end. I'd taken all my finals, handed in my papers, and was as ready for a break as anybody else who'd been pulling all-nighters and cramming in every bit of learning their fried brains could take in up to the last second. I studied through fraternity-funded keggers that went long into the night, until the resident assistants came and threatened to call campus security to shut them down. No matter what, I kept hitting those books until I was overstuffed.

I guess I hadn't paid much attention to what it meant to have the holidays come around, and what I planned to do about them. Thanksgiving had come and gone without much notice. Today, I couldn't for the life of me say where I was, what I ate, and with whom I ate it. For me, it was easy to move right through a holiday as just another ordinary day. Most students stayed around campus for that first Thanksgiving, given we only had two days and a weekend off and no one really wanted to make the drive, or flight, or bus ride, home. Anyway, we were preparing for finals.

Unlike Thanksgiving, my first Christmas break came out of nowhere. I watched as everyone on my floor made their plans, packed their bags, loaded the trunks of their cars up with four to six weeks' worth of clothes— dirty ones mixed with clean—and pillows and blankets to soften the trip home. I listened as my roommate confirmed her flight, discussed the details of celebrating Chanukah with her family, and I heard and felt the crack in her voice as the five months of stored-up homesickness made itself audible. And the first time I was asked where, and with whom, I'd be spending the break, I nearly choked on my own bewilderment.

"Where are you going for Christmas, Regina?" my friend Daula had asked. I had not given it any thought to speak of. I'd arrived on campus, worked hard to stay there. That's all I knew how to do, was be there.

I winged it, gave her what I suspected she wanted to hear. "Oh, home, of course. Texas most likely. And you?"

Where? With whom? What? I'd somehow convinced myself that the dorms would always remain open, that I wouldn't have to worry about needing a place to go, I'd be fine staying on campus by myself, I'd find ways to keep busy, keep myself company.

But as break drew closer, the sounds that seeped through the walls were gone: no phones rang, no televisions or radios blared. The halls were not abuzz with voices. The elevators stood still. I'd promised Tracy to have fun, and that I'd think about meeting her in the Valley, maybe for a long weekend sometime in January, before our break was over. I hadn't traveled anywhere since I'd left Guideways, and I thought a trip some-place, to meet up with someone who'd expect to see me, sounded good.

After I was sure Tracy had gone, I packed up a few things in a backpack and a small orange Samsonite suitcase I'd purchased with my first financial aid check. Just in case one of the RAs came by my room to make sure everyone had checked out, I'd be packed, and they would see that I was just waiting to be picked up. That was the story I'd planned, the lie that momentarily staved off the panic that had reached an all-time high. Also. I'd gone out and purchased as much ramen as a grocery bag could hold. I'd kept bowls, cups, and utensils from the dining hall, and almost everyone had a single-eye hot plate (although they were forbidden), so at least I had something to cook on. Ramen had no smell, so it wouldn't alert anyone that I was there.

Later that night, I heard the elevator stop at my floor, then footsteps headed toward my room. I thought I recognized the person talking to herself out loud, but I couldn't quite make out the words.

"Regina? Girl, where are you?" It was Daula. We'd met in my black studies class. We both got pissed off when our professor, Dr. Laura Head, began preaching about how "all you black girls perming your hair may want to consider how white you all secretly want to be." Daula and I just so happened to protest simultaneously by yelling out, "Uh-uh, I don't think so." But I didn't respond to her knocking at my door, calling out my name. She must not have bought it when I'd told her that I was going to visit my family in Texas.

"I know you're in there, Regina," Daula insisted. "Come on out." I couldn't. I couldn't answer her, or face her. I just could not do it. Next thing I heard was Daula twisting the doorknob, opening the door, and walking in.

"Regina?" she called out. I felt the sting in my eyes and tried to hold back my tears, to hold my breath and bury my body into the corner of the wall to keep from crying, but I could not. I let out a sound of grief so deep, that even as I recall it, hear it, and write it down—in this moment—I feel the same weight of humiliation that I felt when that young woman opened my closet door and saw me sitting there with my things.

"Girl, if you don't get out of that closet . . ." Daula said, in a playful yet challenging way that allowed me a chance to recover gracefully.

Daula invited me home for the holidays, with her. I made a vow to never forget Daula and her kindness, and to repay that kind of generosity to anyone I ever met in need.

Out here on my own

Freshman year segued to sophomore year, and by the time I became a junior, I was as far away from being a disciplined young person as I'd been the day I arrived. It was taking awhile for me to get the hang of what it meant to be an adult, especially regarding money: I struggled to pay my bills on time, and to budget my financial aid award so it stretched an entire year. I used those checks to buy things I'd never had, and desperately yearned for. I bought shoes with pointed toes and shoes with a single strap and Converse in white and Keds with the little blue sticker on the outside just above the sole and Hush Puppies and Birkenstocks and gold Sven clogs and silk and cotton Chinese slippers. If I'd once coveted it, and convinced myself I would become someone desirable if I had it, I bought it.

Each year also brought with it the challenge of finding places to stay over the breaks when the dorms closed, summers included.

Once, while waiting in the laundry room of my dorm waiting for my clothes to dry, I phoned to ask Barbara if she would sponsor me, support me in such a way that all I needed to do was concentrate on getting through my schooling, and provide me with a place to stay. "I already gave at the office," she'd said. The confusion of her response swirled and twirled around my head having no place to land. It took weeks, and my having to repeat that story to anyone who'd listen, before I fully understood its meaning. Not soon enough did it become clear that her sarcasm was possibly a way of sidestepping a request for charity. I was either too naïve to allow Barbara's comment to stick, or I wouldn't have known how to respond to it had I understood it in the moment. Whichever the case, one thing was certain—I didn't have the luxury of letting the shame of it get stuck beneath my skin. In times like that, when it became evident yet again that I was in the world alone, the best way to remedy the reality of the matter was to go out shopping or dancing or drinking; I'd do whatever my mind thought to do in order to get the hurt out of my system. My motto became, *feels good, do it; doesn't feel good, get rid of it*.

There had been a time when I was holding up on a streetlight in front of the GW group home. I was waiting for Gwen to finish a meeting with Barbara relating to a potential new resident, one of her other clients. Barbara had informed Gwen that I would be graduating and moving on, and Barbara wanted to know how she might support me. I was her first resident to ever graduate high school and go on to college. Gwen had cautioned Barbara to be careful of how much support she offered me: "After all," Gwen said, "you don't want her to get accustomed to coming back for more."

That was the thinking back then. Children in foster care were considered adults the moment they turned eighteen, and all things relevant to extended support were out of the question; what we hadn't learned to survive by then was shame on us. Although I'd been granted another year, given I was in school, that extra year hadn't prepared me for anything more than catching up to the fact that I was at a serious disadvantage. We were products of a system that, at that time, had very little data regarding the consequences of forcing us to be on our own before our time. The average American kid has a home with their parents until the age of twenty-five. The average American kid has a seven-year, multiparented, multigenerational advantage over the average foster child. I wonder if anyone was aware that children like me would never, ever, benefit from the collected resources of our parents? We were truly out there on our own.

Eventually, I found my way. I discovered the Career Center at San Francisco State the last quarter of my freshman year, and its various services. I was extremely hopeful the day I came across an ad for the San Francisco Bay Girl Scout Council. They were looking for college students to work as camp counselors. I knew it was the work for me. If hired, not only would I get paid, I'd have a place to stay during the summer, and I'd be able to save the money I made.

I was hired. I enjoyed it so much I returned each subsequent year until I became a counselor-in-training director. Camp was as close as I'd come to feeling like I belonged in the world. I knew that I was there for the kids. I was wild and crazy like many of the campers. I loved making lanyards, and God's eyes, and the group photos we took on the first day. Camp was like the normal childhood I'd never had. I loved learning the songs. My favorite went a little something like this: "Make new friends but keep the old/One is silver and the other's gold . . ."

The first time I learned to make Rice Krispies treats, I ate an entire sheet pan of them. I embraced the value of leaving things better than I found them, which was part of the Girl Scout rules. The Girl Scouts were all about honor. Secretly, I'd always wanted to be involved in the Girl Scouts. More than anything, I wanted that little Brownie dress. There was something about that dress with those pins on it that made me feel that if I could wear it, that somehow, my whole life would change for the better. I would've given my eyeteeth to sell, smell, and taste those cool mint cookies covered in chocolate, all crunchy and delicious, refrigerator cold.

I wonder what their prospects would be like if foster children could have Girl Scout troops dedicated to their plights? I know the answer: they would flourish well beyond their almost-certain limited futures.

Sharp teeth

I'd fulfilled my dream of *getting into* college—but as much as I loved it, *getting out* of college became the problem. Six years after starting, I still hadn't graduated. After my first year, I had a 3.8 grade point average; by the end of my sixth year, I had a 1.7. Looking back, what I needed even more than an education was a place to stay, a home, so I stayed as long as I could get away with it.

In some ways, I was just too embarrassed to graduate. I wanted to. I really wanted to. I just didn't know how I would explain to anyone why there would be no one at my graduation. I had wanted to search for Miss Kerr through all this time, too, but I couldn't face the possibility of not finding her. Better to keep adhering to *feels good, do it; doesn't feel good, get rid of it.*

By 1986, I was twenty-four years old and pregnant. It was a boy. I named him Michael Joseph after the archangel and the father of Jesus. And I was happy. The way I saw it, Michael wouldn't make me have to prove myself. He'd probably never judge me or think badly of me. I'd give him all I ever wanted, and more than he could dream of. He would become my reason for living.

After dropping out of school, and raising my son, I took odd jobs and moved through San Francisco, the world, nomad-like. I needed time to decide what I really wanted to do with my life.

What I had by the time I was in my early thirties was the legacy that I'd lived through, my gorgeous son, a failed marriage to his father, and a decade of experiences, trials, and tribulations that left a wake of wrecked relationships and people in proportions equivalent to what I'd lived through as a child. God, my teeth were far too sharp. The repetitive patterns I'd learned while in care—of not having security, not knowing how to make anything stick, especially the ground beneath my feet—had a life of their own inside of me. I came to understand that I was not at the helm of my life, and thus unable to steer clear of disasters. The time had arrived to do something different. But what?

My new life

"Hello love! Would you like to be a hair model? I need a hair model. I need a black hair model."

1995. I took the white chick's card. It read *Vidal Sassoon*. Their TV commercials touted, "If you don't look good, we don't look good." I agreed to an appointment time and showed up at the salon thinking, *I am about to look good.*

I knew the moment the British girl applied the relaxer onto my scalp and then placed a plastic bag on top of it that I was in trouble. She placed me under a heated dryer and stood by, tapping the time away. I jumped out of that chair, ran to the sink, and started washing my own hair. But the damage was done, and I was left with bald patches and sores. I got a buzz cut and vowed that one day I would get revenge by learning to do all types of hair, and eventually working for Vidal Sassoon.

Which I did.

I worked at Sassoon three years. For every $100 I made for Sassoon, my take was $33 *before* taxes. I cut the hair of up to fifteen clients a day to earn enough for bus fare, childcare, food, and rent.

After several years of just scraping by, I decided to step out on my own with my business partner and start our own salon. My partner's mother was our benefactor and investor.

We were lucky—we got the last suite in the historic Shreve Building just before the dot-commers sent every Bay Area property owner on a money-grubbing rent-hike frenzy. We were in business!

Book Four

Who's who?

By 1988, I'd first reached out to my therapist Lainey at a place called Fort Help to help me learn to save myself. That phone call was a result of viewing a Hallmark commercial. It featured a montage of a father and daughter preparing for the daughter's wedding. She adorns him with nonstop smiles, and he makes it clear, his chest puffed up, how proud he is because of having watched her grow up through all her various developmental stages, which of course are punctuated throughout the commercial. More smiles, hand-holding, hugs, and kisses as he hands her off to her forever love. The weight of my envy became asphyxiating.

But more importantly, I had no idea that some of the side effects of surviving my life appeared to others as jealousy, covetousness, and a silent rage that worked overtime to convince me that mine was a sorry life worth less than the –$3 I had in my overdrawn checking account. There was no such thing as overdraft protection for a life already spent.

I wanted to understand how to be in the world, how to make a way for myself that didn't feel as if it were falling apart at the seams from one relationship to the next, always losing a piece of my fragile sense of self right along with it. I didn't want to keep feeling the brokenness that pulled me out of bed some nights and had me crying for hours like a starving infant for no apparent reason, had me searching, grasping to hold on to somebody, anybody who wouldn't let me go. "You must learn that your love for yourself is the most important, Gina," Lainey said. I didn't know how to wrap my head around that, but what I knew was that I had one hell of a time holding on to myself.

Desperate, I'd engage in means and ways I suspect looked insane to some people, but were methods of survival for me. I'd mimic the actions of anybody I thought worthy of imitating, such as how they talked or presented themselves. I'd heard that imitation was the best form of flattery, so I'd make sure to ask random people if it was all right if I borrowed their behaviors, and usually—if they didn't shoo me off for thinking I might be bordering on creepy—they'd say, "Sure, go ahead." I learned to send thank-you letters; I learned, by observing the manners of doormen and gentlemen on television shows, to hold doors open for the elderly, to greet folks with a smile, even when I really didn't mean it, especially when I didn't mean it. I mastered the skill of acting as if I belonged.

When I was able, I'd even send cards and care packages to Ruby and her two sons. "Kill 'em with kindness," I'd heard someplace. Ruby would receive the gifts and pictures but she'd never call to say she'd gotten anything, or to say thank you. Shame has a way of robbing us of the satisfaction from the very thing we say we want, snatches the good right out of our mouths the moment we get a taste of it. I'd let Ruby convince me that she wanted to be my friend, the way I wanted to be hers. I couldn't leave it at sending her snapshots of the life I was building for myself; no, I had to go in deeper. I thought that if I gave her what she wanted, for someone to take care of her, that she'd love me back in some small way. So, it was easy for me to volunteer to pay Ruby's light bills and phone bills—because for many of my friends, that was a normal thing to do for family members. In my mind, Ruby didn't know any better. No one had taught her to be gracious, thankful. I realized I had to stop it. I didn't know how to give to her without, at minimum, a thank-you. I wanted that acknowledgment from her. So, like breaking a bad habit, I just stopped trying to get a fix from my misguided kindness. I also stopped trying to reconnect with my people, and my past, on their terms.

That Hallmark commercial wasn't the only reason I eventually entered therapy. It also came about from a day when a coworker confronted me.

It had been my first job as a hairdresser. It was a time of having very little funds to purchase the tools of the trade: shears, combs, brushes, a blow-dryer, a cutting cape, neck strips, rollers, and products. These things were essential to the trade. Looking back, I don't know why I did what I did; I just did things on autopilot; my reactions were knee-jerk, impulsive. I'd take my coworkers' combs and brushes and blow-dryers without asking. I might've said, "Let me use this," and before a person could protest, I'd already have it in my busy hands.

One day, a new stylist came to work at our salon. Her name was Candy. Candy had the best tools of anyone, and I really wanted to work with them. So, one day, she placed her blow-dryer in its holder when she was finished drying her client's hair. I picked up the dryer and started using it. The first day I did this, she didn't say much. Perhaps she was intimidated; I was the only black woman in a salon full of white girls, and many times the narrative was they just didn't know how to approach me. Anyway, I kept this up, taking her things and using them as I saw fit.

The day came when Candy'd had it with me. She came into work, her first client sat in her chair, and when she reached for that Beuy Pro number-five comb and that handmade Mason Pearson brush—I loved the way that brush felt in my hands, luxury in motion—and couldn't find what she was looking for, she screamed the door off its hinges.

"Where are my things?" No one said anything. The entire room looked in my direction. I pretended nothing had happened.

From across the room: "You are the most inconsiderate person I've ever met."

Although my insides flew to high alert, I feigned I didn't understand what the fuss was about.

"You have *no* boundaries! You think you can just take anything from anyone anytime you want."

Was it that I didn't know I had to ask? No. That wasn't quite it. I didn't know *how* to ask. I didn't know, and I didn't want to hear anyone tell me that I didn't know in front of everyone. And then there was the truth of my not wanting to hear the word: no. To hear the word *no* felt tantamount to death, disgrace, rejection, dismissal all rolled into one big helping of you're-not-worth-a-damn. I'd rather have the confrontation than the mental ass-whooping I'd get from my own already low self-worth.

I stood in that public humiliation. I was devastated. I couldn't believe I was that dumb.

Learning that I didn't have something called "boundaries" was the final blow that sent me hauling my pulverized ego to Fort Help. After researching at the public library what *boundary* in this respect meant, I was perplexed. I could not understand why I hadn't known better. I faced the mortification head-on and stepped into it to learn its full meaning, as well as how to live beyond my past with a sense of civility, with respectability.

Once, during a session with Lainey many years into my recovery, I asked her, "What am I supposed do with all this healing, all this feeling 'emotionally healthy' about myself?" I was dead serious. I needed to know, now, what good it was going to do to became less dysfunctional, to be more able to stand up for myself. I'd relentlessly scrutinized what had happened in my life, and worked toward a deeper sense of understanding. Time and time again, I reached back into the past, grabbed my demons by the neck, and hauled their squirming asses into the light. And I'd begun to write a little here and there, nothing significant. I brought in a piece of my writing and read it to Lainey, a piece about Big Mama, corn bread, peach-flavored snuff, and Daddy Newt's tobacco pipe.

"Find your mentors, Gina," Lainey said. *Find my what?* I felt duped. (Note to self: look up *mentor*.) All that time and money spent whooping and hollering and remembering things I did not want to remember, experiencing feelings I could have done without feeling, and the best advice she had for me was to go and find something I knew nothing about?

"I don't even know what you're talking about," I told Lainey. "What are mentors?" Thoroughly irritated. Disappointed. Secretly, I just wanted to go home with Lainey. I knew that she lived with her partner and their two children. The youngest was adopted from Nepal. She'd told me, just before she went over there to bring the baby home, that I was the inspiration for the adoption. That no child should be born into the world without someone to care for her. I folded her sentiments into my heart.

"What you read to me was powerful. There must be people, women whose writing inspires you?" Lainey asked, but I couldn't think of anyone I knew personally, in that moment.

"All you need is one person, Gina, someone who'll show you the way to your greatness. Do you know any African American women who you might reach out to?" I didn't think I knew of anyone, nor was that what I wanted to hear. I continued listening. Halfheartedly. I walked out of our session less enthusiastic than I'd arrived. I didn't want a mentor, I wanted Lainey. I wanted Lainey to hold me, hug me, and tell me I was meant to be alive, meant to keep going. I wanted the smell of familiarity, to wrap me in the arms of belonging.

Sometimes Lainey would come and sit next to me, to help me regulate a sudden onset of emotions. "Where did you go?" she might ask. "Who was there with you?" Just her asking me simple questions, sometimes, was enough for me to feel the benefits of being attached, attuned. I came to view her as someone synonymous with caring. "Gina," Lainey said to me one day, "To get emotionally healthy, you're going to need to learn that the love you know as *love* isn't love at all. We're going to need to help you relearn what love means."

The trouble was that getting "healthy" brought with it a host of *needs* I'd never felt I needed, let alone deserved. I needed to hear that I was doing a good job from time to time. I needed to be able to share my dreams with someone, especially someone who'd known me as a child, or teenager, or young adult, and let them see how far I'd come. I wanted, no *needed*, people to tell me how proud of me they were. I'd learned from Lainey that there were other ways to be touched that didn't involve sex.

After some time had passed of working through boundary issues, and learning the differences between my yeses and my nos, I began to understand the importance of where I ended and the world began. This was crucial to my healing. By asking me to find my mentors, I imagined

Lainey was putting my growth to a test, to see if I could truly stand up for myself and become better able to ask for what I wanted from someone, as well as being good with whatever answer they gave given it was their right to do so. I began to understand that the only way through it was to speak up and let my needs be known. It was time to find people, even one person, who could help me practice becoming the new me.

After that meeting with Lainey, I pondered how I'd find (and then ask) a black woman to help me. Barbara was out of the question. I knew she had returned to school as a middle-aged woman, received her master's in social work, and opened at least four more homes. But I had promised myself I'd never ask her for anything unless she first offered. I rarely saw her during those times, and when I did, I never felt deserving of her time.

I'd heard of a book called *Who's Who in America*. A guy I'd had a brief interest in during college had made a big deal out of being in the student version. The book featured the photos, autobiographical highlights, and accomplishments of noteworthy people—artists, political figures, academics, and more. I researched the profiles of three women I'd heard of, whose books I'd read, and in some cases reread:

Maya Angelou—Writer. Activist. Educator. Mother.

Terry McMillan—Writer. Mother.

Alice Walker—Writer. Activist. Educator. Mother.

From the evidence I collected, it appeared that I had at least two things in common with each of these women: I was black and I had one child. I let myself believe that these women were smart about knowing when to stop when it came to having children. One was enough for them, and being a mother hadn't seemed to interfere with their becoming successful writers.

I wrote each woman a letter, asking if she would mentor me as an emerging writer. I didn't see the harm in asking; from the stories I'd heard, such as the ones in my black studies classes during my attendance at San Francisco State, we as black people, overall, came from a rich history of helping one another in times of dire need. I felt proud to know the converse of my own upbringing. Also, I was better able to reframe my relationship with Big Mama after gaining a broader view of the rich heritage of black folks' community. I was better able to consider that, although her caring for me resulted in difficulty and hardship, in the end neither my mother nor her children had been left to fend for themselves on the streets of Austin, Texas. The result of my newly grasped information filled me with the idealist notion that, given the opportunity, most all black people would jump at the chance to help another black person. I believed that I would.

Eventually, I'd come to learn that people were just people, no matter their skin color. They had schedules, and lives; they had to run households, provide for families, friends, and communities. And when someone said no to me, that didn't mean it was personal, about me. It just meant they'd flexed their prerogative to say it. No.

Each writer, in her own way, politely declined to mentor me. It was one of my first exercises in practicing the art of not making their response about me. I chose to view the situation as an occasion to pay tribute instead. I was honored that they had taken the time to even respond. I saw that as a generosity in and of itself. They could've easily left me hanging, waiting and hoping against hope. I embraced my lessons in decorum.

San Francisco, 2002, March 2

Be aware of strangers today. I'd bolted upright in my bed from a crazy dream that had appeared so real that for a split second I was uncertain of who or where I was. I clutched the front of my soaked nightshirt, my heart blasting, as I searched the surroundings, getting my bearings: chest of drawers, photos of my son and me on the nightstand, duvet, all the landmarks in place. Yet and still, the dread clung to me.

Once I'd calmed down and accepted that I'd been dreaming, I glanced over at the clock. It was 9:00 a.m. I jumped out of bed. I had a 9:30 client.

Birdbath behind me, I slammed into my dress and stepped into my heels. Coat. Handbag. I moved like a cheetah on amphetamines down toward 24th and Valencia. Within five minutes, a cab pulsed up beside me. I scurried in and we jetted toward downtown San Francisco. If I were lucky, I'd arrive at my salon by 9:45. My clients were always generous with my being late. I tried not to take advantage.

From the elevator, I glimpsed into the salon as my assistant, Antonio, fluttered about dusting and organizing the front desk. Assuming I had a client waiting, I booked it down the hall.

"Hey Antonio," I said as I rushed in, searching for my client.

"What are you doing here?" he asked. "Didn't you get my message?"

"No, what message?" I asked, catching my breath.

"Sarah cancelled, girl. She had to reschedule for another day."

Great! What a relief! I had enough time to catch up for my next client, who would be arriving within the next half hour. I picked up the printed-out schedule and stared at the long, blank columns. Tony must have read the expression on my face.

"If you'd listened to my message, Miss Thing, you could've saved yourself a trip—*and* the embarrassment of having your dress on inside out," he said, laughing. I loved Tony. He made a day of standing on my feet—in impractical shoes, having to cut, color, weave, and/or style one client after the next—go by in love and laughter.

"You could've given me the $25—plus tip—you paid for that cab ride."

He sensed my confusion.

"Girl, your whole day fell apart somewhere between midnight and dawn! Even crazy Sherry, who begged you to fit her in so you could tighten her weave, left a message that she had to cancel, no money, she said."

"I'll tell you what," I said, suddenly inspired. Something inside of me was pushing me to leave as quickly as I'd rushed in. "Call and confirm my clients for Saturday, and then reschedule the ones who've requested an appointment for next week. Give anyone who asks my lunch hour on whatever day they want it. I'll come in early and stay later. After all that, Tony, just go home and we'll call it a day. Oh—and please call my son and see if he's coming home this weekend, I need to know if I'm picking him up."

"All right, then, girl. I'll leave you a message on your phone. Make sure you check those messages!"

I exited the lobby of the Shreve Building at 210 Post Street and traveled east into the wind. Earlier, when running to catch the taxi, I hadn't noticed the blustery weather. I buttoned my jacket against the cold and headed toward the Barnes & Noble bookstore on Union Square.

Still curious to find my mentors, I'd scoured the internet for writers who'd written about incredibly challenging childhoods. I'd read Maya Angelou's memoir, Ruthie Bolton's *Gal*, and happened upon Dave Pelzer. I took the escalator to the second floor, where the nonfiction was kept, grabbed Pelzer's *A Child Called "It"*, purchased it, and hoofed it toward the Powell Street BART station. Through Union Square, I jetted past

Chanel, Macy's, Neiman Marcus, too cold to slow down. I made a hard right and rattled down the steps leading underground to the station.

The loudspeaker announced that the approaching train was headed to Daly City. I strode through the crowd, rammed my ticket into the slot, pushed through the turnstile, took the escalator two steps at a time, and glided onto the train just as the doors closed.

I took an empty seat beside a woman holding her daughter. Briefly, I watched as the mother, a dark-skinned Latina with a bright smile, swept, gently with her fingertips, the sleeping child's hair across her forehead. Into the little girl's ear, she murmured words, whose meanings were meant for the little girl alone.

I thought about my own little boy. How off and on, between the ages of five and thirteen, he went in and out of wanting my help, needing my love. Every book I read by baby/child experts like Brazelton and Spock had tried to prepare me—intellectually—for the developmental stages and the changes they promised, but nothing could've prepared me for the actual experiences. Michael was the poster child for strong-willed. He wasn't one to give love up too easily. He required much in terms of patience and acceptance. He made sure I worked for his love. Given that relational interactions live in the subjective realm: I can only pray I've done well by him.

However, as a small boy from three years old to maybe seven, I found it was easiest to gush my mama love over Michael while he slept, or when he was ill. It was then, and usually only then, that I could touch him without being accused that my touch, no matter how tender, hurt his skin or his hair. No place on his body welcomed my well-intended tenderness. If I pushed the issue, or tried holding him longer than he preferred, the result was an all-out temper tantrum. "Get your hands off me," his flailing little arms and hands seemed to say. Hugs were out of the question. Five pediatricians all confirmed the same suspicions: Mike was angry. The divorce made it so he had to go back and forth between his dad and me. He hated it. In the early years after his dad and I divorced, I insisted that Michael visit his father on weekends. My rationale was that I didn't want to be blamed, later, for impeding their relationship. Michael always resisted. Too invested in trying to right the wrongs of my own childhood experience, I failed to listen to him. I paid the price of that failure each time he withdrew his love.

I held the space. Gladly. "He'll come back to you later," is what my friends, clients, and therapist assured. I willed myself to wait for his return.

The shrieking sound of train wheels snapped me back from my reverie. I'd arrived at my stop—24th and Mission. I stood and waited for the woman, still carrying the girl, to step out of the way.

Once on the platform, I headed for the stairs. That's when the stranger passed me. He had the sort of face that women never forget: a broad forehead, smooth skin, hazel-green eyes. He was stunning. I turned and started after him.

"Hey! Hey, you," I said to the man in the too-short-sleeved overcoat. He slowed his stride but did not stop. He turned his head slightly and looked right through me. His gaze unsteady. He turned and kept going.

"Excuse me," I said, this time louder, waving wildly. I must've sounded slightly panicked—several people turned to see if I was speaking to them, their faces full of quiet consternation. I hurried toward the man. He stopped and turned toward me.

"You talking to me?" he asked.

"Yes, I am," I said, moving in closer to him, hardly believing his question.

"You speak to me as if I should know you," he replied. Up close, his beige skin was slightly lined. Although there was a two-inch-wide bald spot that stretched from his forehead to his nape, splitting what was left of his hair into matted Afro puffs on either side of his head, he didn't look a day over fifty years old. He did however, look a bit like Homey the Clown. Small beads of perspiration melted down his temples. He shivered ever so slightly. The closer I stood to him, the more I inhaled light, musky whiffs of wet dirt, cocktailed with traces of an unnamable men's cologne.

"Are you saying you don't remember me?" I asked, and did a quick mental check of my hair, makeup, and double-breasted Marc Jacobs trench coat. I felt good about how I looked, at least.

"Why should I remember *you?*"

"My name is . . . Regina." I said in an incriminating way, brow heavy with skepticism.

"My, what a fine name, Regina, but I am sorry, I don't believe we've ever met. Why should I know you?" I felt a surge of terror rush through me. I couldn't imagine that *this* was how God had ever intended for my life to be. I swallowed.

"I am your daughter, Tom. My mother is Ruby."

As I stood there, waiting for that stranger to recall our connection, I couldn't help but think about the Ten Commandments, specifically the one about honoring thy mother and father. I'd made it so easy for them over the years. Not wanting to run them even farther gone than they already were, I never asked for anything. I didn't sweat them with why they hadn't tried to get to know my son—or me, for that matter. I'd honored them the best way I knew how: by leaving them and the past of it all behind, and for what? There I stood, staring my past in the face, and my past couldn't recognize me. For a short moment, I took that *very* personally.

But then that passed. It was as if my ability to understand the situation cracked open, and I suddenly realized that I'd waited my entire life to stand this man down and tell him how I really felt. The longer I stood there, in silence, the better able I was to hold on to that smallest part of myself, the one that had dreamed of perforating his eyeball sockets with an ice pick, the part that loathed him for never loving me into calling him "Daddy," the feral and ravenous part of me that still suffered over how he'd just walked away, turned his back. Just. Like. That. For years, I'd had visions of running into him, of how I would use every profanity I'd ever heard to curse and shame him all the way back to his mother's womb.

I stood there. Quietly. Holding myself. He spoke.

"Ain't God good! Ain't it good to see you still amongst the living?"

I was shocked. It was a challenge to believe what that man was saying to me. It was as though his body was here, but whatever spoke from him was from another realm. When I had last seen Tom, maybe fifteen years before that moment, during a visit to his little house on Downer Street, I'd learned about the time Barry White had sacked him. According to him, Barry had felt concerned that his protégé's album would catapult him—Tom—to the top of the charts. Barry felt threatened, was Tom's version. Tom had sneered nonchalantly, claiming that he was composing songs for another record. That time I'd seen him, and I was barely twenty-one, and the house felt especially empty, I'd asked how his wife Nadine and their three children were doing. He said that he'd locked Nadine in the closet where she belonged. Their son was allergic to her. Their son was asthmatic. I left within a breath of hearing the story. As insane sounding as it was, Tom appeared more coherent then, less otherworldly.

"Why did you leave me, Tom?" I didn't wait for an answer.

"Why did you let me bounce all over the place like that? Thirty different placements? How come I needed to go through all that, when I had you? Most of those people didn't even want to see me coming. Remember Miss Kerr, that white lady who wanted me? Why didn't you just sign me over to her? I was locked up in an institution, Tom. You knew that. In solitary confinement! I was forced to take all kinds of drugs. *Why didn't you come for me?*"

Tom's stare bored right through me.

"You're the one who abandoned me," he finally managed to say through his apparent trance. He had my attention, and had I been a braver-cum-vindictive girl, I would've pushed him straight into an oncoming train. From that point forward, I didn't see a way to go on with Tom, to try to make sense out of our past, to give him a chance to own his part, to say something, to be generous no matter how gratuitous it may've been.

"I've been working down at 16th and Mission near the donut shop," Tom said. "I'm getting the whores ready for Jesus's return. He is on his way back, you know?" Still caught up on the bramble of him accusing me of abandoning him, I worked hard to breathe my way through it, to get present. I tried to follow what he was saying only to realize: *Tom wasn't with me.* I'd experienced enough in my own treatment to know when someone had split off. I'd split off myself, many times, when things became too painful to face.

I reconsidered how Tom looked, the story appearance told. The duct-taped jacket, backpack, shoes. If I'd allowed myself to feel, in that moment, the full weight of that assessment, it would've been absolutely and undeniably heartbreaking. I couldn't do that. I could not go to heart-break. I'd spent far too much time there; it was my turn to let myself off that hook, my time to be my own fucking father. I muffled a moan. Instinctively I knew not to cry, not with him. I took a breath and counted to ten.

And without warning I wanted to reach out to Tom. I wanted to grab him, kiss him, and hold him and say to him that *I am here, it's me, your daughter, Regina. Everything is gonna be all right.* I wanted to grip hold of his enormous cracked hands; those same hands had once taught me how to hold a tennis racket, and how to get a live worm onto a fishing pole and cast the fishing line into the water. He taught me how to reel in the catch. In that moment, though, I did not know how to reel Tom in and simultaneously release him.

"There's something I want to give you before you die." The words, un-rehearsed, fell from my mouth. For the first time, Tom looked up at me, as if he understood what was coming next.

"I forgive you, Tom," I said, "For not showing up for yourself." I paused. "You are no longer my earthly keeper. I release you. You are free to go."

We both stood there clumsily in the emptiness. And even though, in some small way, the exchange didn't feel totally clean, I was willing to live with that. Neither of us had expected that encounter. And I could see that the man I once knew as my birth father had been replaced by some-thing else, another disaster that I hadn't shared in the making of. For that

I was grateful. I could see that our chance meeting was nothing more than an opportunity to meet Tom's ghost, to reconcile my own need to speak into the void, and cleanse myself of the beliefs I carried. No matter what I'd done to make myself more successful, more stylish, more beautiful, and more whole, my people, my father, my mother, were never coming for me in the way I'd hoped they would. But what was possible, that day, is that my father's ghost had given me a chance to hear myself say it out loud: *I forgive you.* That was for me. I turned and headed for the escalator.

"Wait!" Tom's voice pulled me back around. I waited. Listened.

"I got diabetes," Tom said. "The doctor says I'm doing well. I don't take their poison—insulin. I got God. Anyway, the doc says that I'm doing just fine."

In that moment, I saw a shining innocence, an excitement in his eyes. It was as though he was no more than an unknowing and inquisitive boy standing before his third-grade class on show-and-tell day. He seemed so pleased with himself. I half expected him to pull the diabetes, like a pet lizard or a bag of marbles, out of the raggedy, duct-taped backpack and hold it up for the entire class to see.

"Great! I mean, thank you, it's nice to finally know something about my family history." I turned to leave again.

"Wa . . . it." This time, Tom's voice wasn't as strong. It cracked. "Don't you want my phone number?" Still seeing the young boy, I took the number he'd scribbled onto an old BART ticket and stuffed it in my pocket.

I fell in step with a small crowd that had just disembarked a train.

"Wait!" Tom yelled again.

I stopped.

"How did you know it was me, Regina?" The incomprehensibility of Tom's question punched me like a battering ram. How could I *not* know? That was my father. For Christ's sake. *My father.* I decided to close the situation down. There'd be no more secret hoping, dreaming, or rationalizing that one day my father might suddenly change, and want me.

"That's the work you get to do, Tom."

Mystified, I stepped onto the jam-packed escalator. From the corner of my eye, I managed to sneak a peek and see, if by some shred of a chance, Tom might be watching after me. No surprise, he was not. He could not. I kept my eyes fixed on him. My father slowly picked up his backpack and with both hands clasped it to his chest. I watched him disappear into the crowd on the train platform.

Once outside, I stood on the concrete pavement where 24th Street intersects Mission Street. I was four blocks from home. I began to tremble. It felt as if I hadn't seen Tom, and was never going to see him again. I felt as if I'd revisited a trauma, one that had been lurking in the shadows, awaiting its turn to step into the light, and as a result I was spinning, triggered, stunned. Punch-drunk. I literally stumbled toward home.

I somehow imagined

On the second block, the outline of a neon-red martini glass with a green olive affixed to the rim pushed through the heavy mist. I wasn't big on drinking, but the idea of it struck me as a solid alternative to the guilt-bashing that was going on inside my head. Resisting the urge provided a momentary distraction.

I turned onto my street, San Jose Avenue. I felt an overwhelming desire to blame myself for Tom not recognizing me. The next thing I wanted to do was punish myself, hurt myself. That way, I wouldn't have to wait another ten, fifteen, maybe thirty years to confront anyone in the hopes of forging a reunion. That way, I'd be the perpetrator deserving of being left. That way, there'd be no one else to hold personally culpable.

If I was that same girl I had been before—the fifteen-year-old me—I imagined I would've asked a counselor for one of the pink Daisy razors they handed out at Edgar Children's Shelter. I would've slammed the razor onto the bathroom floor until the blade popped out. And I would've cut my wrist crosswise to the vein.

Frantically, I pushed through the door of my flat, wringing my hands, wondering what to do next. I needed to call someone. Lainey and I had created a system: should anything ever become overwhelming in between our sessions, I could call her answering machine and leave a message. Sometimes I called when I attended other people's family events. The happiness, familiarity, and hugging and kissing would become too much for me. Conversationally, I never felt I had anything appropriate to bring to the mix when it came to—and it always came to—where I was from, what about my family, how did I grow up? Those were the usual variables that made up the average dinner party conversations I'd participated in. My situation was not my friend's fault.

I thought to call my mother, Ruby. I somehow imagined that time and distance might've calmed her, softened her defenses, and as a result she'd be able and willing to hear me, to understand how running into Tom might affect me. She'd maybe say, "Now, now, Baby."

I wanted someone to *explain* to me what I was experiencing. I didn't want to be the one, again, steeling up, acting as if I did not need any support. I didn't have the strength to understand, and/or turn my goddamned-fucking cheek. What about me? Who was supposed to care for me?

Even if I had her phone number, Ruby would never be a good choice.

I thought of which one of my friends I could call, but I didn't know anyone who knew I'd had a family, once. And there it was again, that ambiguous loss, taking credit for the moment.

"Hello, Lainey," I spoke into the phone, "It's Gina. I just wanted you to know I ran into my father, Tom, today. I guess I'm okay. I—uh . . . just wanted to tell somebody." Phone receiver back in cradle, I went back to wringing my hands, wondering what to do, how to feel? I paced back and forth between the hallway and my bedroom. I was glad my son wasn't home. I wouldn't have wanted him to see me so out of my body, or need to explain the situation.

Slowly, I came to recognize that the less I resisted the confusion, the easier it became to befriend the emotional ambush, the chaos roiling inside of me. With acceptance came relaxation. Then, after a long silent while, there came an instant where I felt that anything was possible if I just believed it to be.

Find a piece of paper, a voice said from within. It was just like that. Not one to be told what to do, I resisted. My mind flashed between images of razor blades and alcohol.

Find a piece of paper, now, the voice demanded. I did a cursory check through the entryway-table drawers, relieved to have tried, yet failed.

I walked into the living room. A copy of the *Bay Guardian* sat on top of several *Sunset* magazines. I picked up the newspaper.

Find a pencil. Back to the entryway table I went, thrashing through drawers, until I found a pencil, my heart strangling inside my chest.

Sit down. I sat down on the edge of my rocking chair, pencil perched. Like a Ouija board planchette, my pencil began to ramble around the edges of the delicate newspaper. My hand moved, recording the images that flashed across my mind.

I lost track of time, but remained acutely aware of the energy that pulsed through me; it was if I were sprinting the last leg of a race, trying to get across that finish line first. I traveled back in time through Texas. I saw Big Mama and Lula Mae. Lula Mae leaned from her bedroom window, calling for me to find her babies' socks and onesies that the storm winds had blown off the clothesline, or else.

I looked down at what I had written. I was a mixture of scared and excited: scarecited.

Careful not to disturb the raggedy screen door that barely kept the man-eating mosquitoes from tearing our asses up, I leaned my body into the frame and stared up at the sky. I could tell by the way the clouds moved that God was gonna start crying soon. I wondered who had pissed the angels off this time. The white lady from the Church of the Nazarene told me that whenever somebody committed a cruel act against one of God's children, their guardian angel would run and tell Him, and He would cry for their pain—that's where raindrops come from. The white lady said that when the clouds changed quickly from fluffy white to smoky gray, well, that's when the angelic messengers were running across the heavens. And when every breath you take holds the promise of His tears mixing with the dirt, it was guaranteed to be a grand event. Thunder! Lightning! And sometimes if the crime was unforgiveable, He might just throw golf balls made of ice at them. I know one thing: I felt sorry for whoever it was this time, but I sure was glad it wasn't me.

———

"Gi . . . nna, come on in," Lainey said. Her smile was wide, prairie wide. I loved the way my insides warmed whenever I was in Lainey's company. Mostly. I followed her down the short hall into her room. I entered while Lainey bent over and turned on the sound diffuser that sat just outside the door. I could always count on Lainey for consistency. Her room felt warm and safe from one week to the next, everything in place, nothing ever changing. Feeling especially vulnerable, I picked up a beige throw, wrapped myself into a bundle, and cuddled into the middle of her sofa. She'd given me permission to meet my own needs as I saw fit.

The first meeting I'd had with Lainey, I asked if she understood emotional distresses that came in varying shades, or if she was only for and about white people's troubles. She'd laughed. I eyed the books that crowded her shelves. I loved how close they were, cover to cover, their spines vertical. I checked off the ones that were familiar to me, that I'd either already read before meeting Lainey or that I'd gone out and purchased over the thirteen years that I'd been working with her: *Seat of the Soul, The Road Less Traveled, Sacred Contracts, Home Coming: Reclaiming and Championing Your Inner Child, Man's Search for Meaning*. I had a habit of looking for new ones. I wanted to know what she knew. I wanted to never be without the tools to help myself.

Lainey, giant water glass in hand, eased into the dark brown leather recliner. The footrest sprang up and there I sat, staring at the waffled bottoms of her "therapist clogs." They were always a dark color, burgundy or brown, and matched her overly bright outfits, which were equally absent of style.

I sat for a while, staring at the table clock. Timex. Lainey had gray-blue eyes that felt as if they never left my face during our fifty-minute sessions. If I looked at her she'd smile, and sometimes I smiled, too. But that day, I wasn't smiling so much as I didn't know how to start. Whenever I felt choked up in our sessions, wordless, I'd convince myself that it was *my* time, after all, and I could do with it what I pleased. That's the thing about paid-for relationships: I could have the first and last say in how things were done.

"How does it feel to be here, Gina, on a day we don't usually meet?" Lainey asked.

"Fine, I guess," I said.

"What brings you in today?"

"You know. I left it on your answering machine." My teeth clamped down. *Is she really going to make me work for this?*

"You want to talk about the message you left?"

Duh!

I inspected my fingers. Picked at my cuticles.

I opened my mouth but the words got stuck. I'd hoped to be better for the incident of running into Tom. I'd done so good on that platform, hearing him, making space, working hard to not take it personally. But somewhere between leaving him, getting home, and the writing, I'd lost a bit of my courage. I couldn't find *that* adult who'd stood up to Tom. I looked over at Lainey. She forced the footrest back into place and scooched two or so feet in front of me.

"Point to where it's stuck, Gina." I'd agreed to let Lainey address me by my favorite name. It was the one I liked best from childhood, the one thing to keep what was good about that time in my life.

"He ... didn't ... know ... me." I managed to say through the hiccups, the appalling indignation of it all. I hadn't realized it, but the grief had taken on epic proportions between the incident with Tom and making it to the appointed time with Lainey. Without my suspecting, it had taken up residence in my throat.

"Who didn't?"

"My fa—Tom—didn't ... know me."

"How does that make you feel, Gina?" In that moment, I didn't know how I felt; everything ran together into one long smear. I suddenly felt self-conscious, as if I were being viewed as a crybaby or coward.

"I don't *feel* anything," I said sarcastically. "How would it feel if I punched you in the face?" I asked.

I wanted to scream, claw at her, punch her in the face again and again and again. I wanted to tear off all my clothes and run screaming bloody murder out of the window. I wanted her to stop asking bonehead questions she already knew the answers to.

"Plant your feet on the ground, Gina," Lainey instructed. Taking my time, I uncurled from my position and did as I was instructed. She leaned a little closer and asked me if I'd like to put my hands in a more comfortable position. I sat on them. My shoulders hunched. My feet turned in.

"How old are you right now?"

"Thirty-eight. Why?" I said, further irritated: *How the fuck is this helping me? What does it matter how old I am right now?*

"How old—"

"I'm fifteen, okay?" I said. "Fif-fucking-teen."

"What happened after you ran into Tom?"

"I went home."

"Then what did you do?"

"I, uh, called your machine and left a message."

"Did you do anything else?"

"No, but I wanted to . . . I wanted to . . . hurt . . . myself."

"How would you have hurt yourself, Gina?"

"I wanted to push my naked body through a tight wall of rosebushes till all there was left were pieces of me, shredded like cheese!" I panted. "I wanted to bleed what I feel out of my body, bleed the want of my mama and daddy out . . . of . . . my . . . body."

"Yes, Gina," Lainey said. "Go on," she encouraged. Her eyes locked on my face. The depth of my distress began to show in the collapsing expressions that took over her face; the space between her brows pleated, her lips pursed, eyes watered.

"Something told me to not hurt myself," I said, wiping the snot on the sleeve of my shirt. "It was like when I was in solitary confinement and I was able to get to calm, stay there, and give another option a chance to show up."

"Gina, the harm that you wanted to do to yourself is the hurt you've been carrying around . . . for years, the hurt that was possibly done when you were preverbal," Lainey said. I watched as tears hovered in the rims of her eyes.

"I wrote it all down," I said, absentmindedly.

"You wrote what down, Gina?" Lainey asked. She wiped her face with a tissue, and then placed the box on the floor between us. "You mean you wrote down what happened last Friday at the BART station, between you and Tom?"

"Yeah."

"How was it, to write that?" Lainey asked.

"Fine, I guess. I'm not sure of what to do with it," I said.

"Gina, we have just a few minutes before we need to end." That was the part I despised the most about therapy. Just when the going was getting good, our time was up. I didn't move. I stared into space.

"Where are you now Gina?" Lainey asked. I wanted more time. Even after all the years of being together, it was still difficult to ask for what I needed.

"Would you like a hug?" she asked. Not wanting to come across as a charity case, I hesitated. I was afraid that if I let her hug me, she'd have to call someone to pry my fingers loose.

I stepped into her embrace, anyway.

Next door to Lainey's office building was an alcove. On many days, after a session, and when I wasn't quite ready to fold back into my life, the world, I'd nestle into that nook to ease my way back to the present. That day, Lainey was only ten minutes behind me. From where I stood, I watched as she strode across the street, confidently. I wondered where she was headed. To pick up her daughters? To meet her lover? I wondered what it would be like to come home to her, as a friend, a sister, a mother? As I pushed away from that wall, that day, and headed back into my own life of being friend, lover, and mother, I took with me the silent, sweet knowing that Lainey, in her efforts to model what a different kind of love looked like, had been my very own miracle worker.

My lithium should be kicking in ...

"Hi. I'm Regina," I said, extending my hand. I turned the chair around so that we could both get a solid look at ourselves in the mirror. "What can I do for you today?"

Through the mirror I watched and listened while Marybeth made her best effort to describe the hairstyle she'd seen on a woman in Santa Fe. She pulled a clump of magazine pages from her heavily fringed silver and turquoise purse.

"Oh, great, you brought pictures," I said.

"Yes indeed," she said, "I tore 'em from an old issue of *Vogue* on the plane ride back to California."

Marybeth, it turned out, had a second home in Santa Fe, someplace I'd long wanted to visit. I'd heard other friends, and clients, speak of how "magical" and "mystical" of a place it was, especially for women.

"May I have a glass of water, please?"

"Absolutely. I'm so sorry for the oversight, that's usually the first thing we offer."

"Oh, don't worry about it," Marybeth insisted. Antonio, the finest eavesdropper on the planet, handed her a cold bottle of spring water before I asked.

"My lithium should be kicking in any minute now," Marybeth said as Tony led her from the shampoo bowl to the cutting chair. "I forgot to take it this morning, with the traveling and so forth." Tony and I exchanged quick glances. I could hear him through the silence thinking, *What?* I knew better than to give him another second to poke the bear.

"Did you just say you're on lithium bicarbonate?" I hadn't met anyone since I'd left Guideways who had so openly disclosed they were on meds. "I was on that as a teenager," I said, adrenaline scorching through me.

"That's surprising," my client replied, her face suddenly wide-awake with curiosity. "They don't normally put kids on drugs like that. What was going on?"

"I was sixteen. I lived in a residential treatment center." I wasn't a stranger to confiding certain parts of my life to my clients. Over the years I'd become deft at cherry-picking the moments I'd lived through that related to theirs. I'd learned over time that people become leery of those whose lives or experiences feel too different from their own.

"They must've thought you were in a pretty bad way to put you on lithium. That is no small drug to mess with," Marybeth went on. "Why were you on it?"

"I'm still trying to figure that out," I answered, not wanting to go all the way into it.

"Well," Marybeth said, "I understand what you mean, and I thank God every day for Jane, my writing coach."

"What do you mean?" I asked. Suddenly very curious.

"She helps me write so that I can better understand what I've experienced." She went on to explain that once a month she met with a writing instructor who worked out of the extension at the university over in Berkeley.

"Oh," I said, completely intrigued.

"I'll write down her name for you if you think you're interested?"

"I'd love that!" I said.

That was the first and last time I ever saw Marybeth Warren.

The arm of an eight-year-old

It didn't take long for me to call Jane Anne Staw. I wasn't sure of my intentions in contacting her, but whatever it was she did with Marybeth, I wanted to know more about it.

A week or so prior to running into Tom, I'd taken Lainey's advice and begun writing down some of the memories we'd discussed during our sessions. The first experience that came to mind was my relationship with Miss Kerr. I'd thought about her many times over the years. I even remembered her birthday, August 15. Countless times on that date, through the years, I'd stop what I was doing, wonder how she was, where she was, and with whom she was living her life. I'd wish her a silent happy birthday. Nobody ever spoke the words *Sweetheart* and *Punkin'* to me the way she had.

"Please send me what you've got," Jane requested. I told her I only had five pages, and explained to her the circumstances under which they had been written. She reiterated that she wanted whatever I had. *I did it!* I shouted out loud, as I hung up the phone. Someone was interested in at least reading what I had to say and I'd had the courage to reach out. *Yes!*

I sent Jane my best—and only—five pages. Three weeks slowly crept by before I decided to call and check in with her. I knew nothing about protocol and not bugging folks when it came to the literary world and all its machinations. According to her outgoing message, though, Jane was on a monthlong "nesting" retreat with her newly adopted daughter. I resolved to wait it out.

The more I dipped into my memories, the more I began to question what *I thought* had happened versus what had *actually* happened. Could I trust the images that flashed into my mind, the pipe smell that came along with the mention of Daddy Newt's name, or the taste of cold watermelon doused with salt that filled my mouth at the mention of summers in Texas? The crystal-clear scene when Ruby visited me and my sister, and promised I could leave with her come morning? Had it really happened?

In that scene, I followed the arm of an eight-year-old as she moved with fierce determination, clutching a Safeway bag. The swinging arm approached the driver's side of an automobile, placed the bag on the ground, opened the door to my mother's car, a 1970-something bur-gundy Cutlass Supreme. I pushed the driver's seat forward, and placed the bag holding what I believed to be my belongings into the back seat. I remembered thinking: *I'm gonna put my bag here, so that way Ruby won't forget and leave without me.* The power and conviction I felt had never left me, I thought; it had haunted me up to the time I began writing. Or had it? I wasn't so certain anymore; but the emotional truth of what I began to write felt right.

"Hi, Regina, it's Jane. Sorry it's taken me so long to get back to you. As you may remember, I have a new family member—"

"Hello?" I ran from my bedroom half naked and snatched up the re-ceiver.

"Hey," Jane said. "Listen, I'd love to work with you. I think you have an amazing voice. It's refreshing, actually."

"Oh—okay," I said, suddenly confused. "But you've never heard me sing."

I think we were both confused, judging by the moment of silence that followed my confession. Then Jane laughed gut-hard, followed by a conciliatory "Ahh—" as she understood.

"No, that only means, in writerly language, that you have a way of telling your story that's memorable," she said. I remained confused, but that didn't matter; I had found someone willing to help me.

"Can you afford $60 an hour?"

I could. "When do we start?" I asked.

"Wednesday, next week," Jane said.

"Congratulations on your new daughter!" I said. "What country did you get her from?" I imagined that, like a couple of my friends, she had gone to either Guatemala, China, or Russia.

"Ha!" Jane said laughing. Again. "Daphne Opal is a dog. She's my new girl." In the background, a dog barked.

Each week that Jane and I met brought with it a host of emotional ghosts, or "grief pockets," as I called them. Memories rolled in, sometimes in full scenes, sometimes in slivers or fragments that might arise out of something I touched, like the pull on a chrome-beaded light chain. That recollection came back as:

I am in a room. It's dark. There are several large windows; headlights roll across the walls and ceiling. A cigarette smell, a high-pitched laugh, a man, a door slamming. A child (I don't know how old) screaming. The child walking against traffic, headlights blinding her . . .

I could not string that moment together with any other, although I had felt it so deep in my body that, somehow, I had seen what *that* child, the one in the memory, had also witnessed.

Each week I eagerly looked forward to what I referred to as "Wednesdays with Jane." Every session, which took place on the heels of my meetings with Lainey, began with me reading the pages I'd written over the previous week. That time was spent widening, deepening, and what Jane called *polishing* the narrative. Those times became my safe place to allow my people from Texas to visit. Their forgetting me, and my speculations that perhaps they had never existed—a denial evident in the fact that I'd never discussed them with my son or anyone else—slowly became easier to confront. Before long, I found happier moments about my childhood: the cookouts at Big Mama's, how my sister and I pretended we were Freda Payne and sang "Band of Gold," how my sister told me I reminded her of the snowbird in Anne Murray's song by the same name, and how she sang it to me sometimes, nights when we were both too hot to fall asleep.

Soon enough, I came to recognize that my haircutting skills, which I'd spent years honing, weren't so unlike those skills needed to whittle down a chunk of white-hot emotion into something touchable. It all came down to developing the patience to craft matter into a different kind of thing. What I didn't realize at first was how the writing was working upon me. How, the more I faced my traumas, looked at them dead-on, and remained willing to befriend and therefore transform them, the more space I created within myself. The lighter I felt. The better I slept. The happier I became. Soon enough, I was aware that there was something in the creation that was bigger than me, better able to discern right from wrong, bad intentions from good ones; and as I realized that, I was also able to see that what was out there—the bigness, the beauty, the generosity of spirit—was also inside of me. Life began to mirror my possibilities.

It was on the tail end of that recognizing that Jeanne came in. Although I'd searched for her from time to time, I hadn't let anyone else know I was doing so—not even Lainey. I'd gone so far as to order phone books from as many states as I could—as far away as Hawaii and as close as Colorado—but my ceaseless phone calls had shown no results.

The first time Jeanne showed up in my writing, she came in a yellow jumpsuit. Or was it denim? I couldn't be certain if the jumpsuit she had worn was yellow, back then in the late seventies, but that is the color that came with the memory. Her voice called out to me, "Sweetheart," in that familiar way, and I saw that root-beer-brown hair of hers in ropey whorls. Lord. I didn't share her with Jane, at first; I didn't share her with anyone. I wanted to keep her for myself.

Initially Jane helped me steer the narrative toward my being a foster child who'd bounced from home to home and how the system had "failed" me. That approach felt too victim driven for my tastes.

I did some research in 2000, and to my surprise, there were very few memoirs written for or about black women at that time. I wanted to say something that spoke to why there were so many more black children in foster care, proportionally, than in the general population. I felt we needed a different way to enter into the story. If no one was paying attention to all those children floating in society's blind spot, they probably wouldn't pay much notice to a story bringing attention to that fact. That's when I began to share Jeanne with Jane. In some ways, losing her had been so devastating from a systematic perspective that I couldn't—as a child—fully comprehend the weight of her presence or her absence.

"I can't believe you've been holding out on me!" Jane said. "That *is* your story. My God! That's your story. Of course . . . She was your mother, the first real mother you ever had, and you lost her. She lost you. No wonder you haven't shared her."

Our plan

In December of 2000, Jane explained to me what an agent was and decided it was time for me to get one. I'd spent the previous five months calling up local bookstores and offering to read from my "work in progress." I loved saying that, "work in progress," the infinity of it; the idea that there would always be work to be done felt comforting. It made me feel as if I'd always have something of my own if I had my writing. I'd invite my clients to attend my readings at Barnes & Noble stores from Berkeley to Richmond to Walnut Creek. I read at Borders Books in Pleasant Hill. I read at any and all literary events I could get myself involved with. I even managed to get several local newspapers to write articles about my upcoming memoir. I visualized a publisher having already acquired my book; I could see it in the bookstore before it was even there. The fact that I could attract between fifty and 200 audience members to listen to me tell a story that was not yet bound in a sellable manuscript was encouraging to bookstore owners, to Jane, and most of all, to me.

Our plan was to send out the first fifty pages. Jane described how, with a nonfiction manuscript, we'd only need to send a portion of the book along with a book proposal. The idea was to send a query letter out to as many agents as we liked, and hook them into asking to see the book proposal; from there they'd hopefully fall in love with my story. Then, one of the agents would use his or her connections with editors and publishers, and the next thing we hoped for was a book deal between me and whichever party was most interested in publishing my book. "I think it's time for you to try and find Jeanne," Jane said. "You should know if she's still alive. She might be able to fill in parts you can't remember."

Someone's Somebody

Time came around to where I needed a title. At that time, I just so happened to be reading a collection of vignettes by Gloria Naylor called *The Women of Brewster Place*. In giving so much of my time over the years to becoming a mother and a business owner, I hadn't done very much reading. In an effort to know something more about the lives of black folks other than the people I came from, I began reading what called out to me. It was in that book's first chapter, "Mattie Michael," that I came across the phrase "someone's somebody." The character Mattie had gone searching for her son, who'd been jailed. I felt the plea in those two words, what it was to love someone who could not love you back. But at least with Jeanne, I knew that she had wanted me, once, and her wanting me had made me feel like I was someone's somebody.

It took an entire week to write a query letter. Jane advised that given the amount of these letters agents and editors received, I had to craft one that would *not* end up in a *slush pile*, the place where most unsolicited letters of inquiry found themselves.

I emailed my first query letters on April 28, a few days before my thirty-ninth birthday, and right before embarking on a seven-day cruise. Upon returning I found an email from an agent Jane had recommended. I couldn't believe it. The excitement of reading the email's subject line: "I LOVE your voice. I am completely interested in discussing further . . ." was one of the most exciting things I'd ever experienced.

I sat down at my desk and read it again. And again. I leaned back in my chair trying to picture what I'd say to someone interested in representing my story about the little black girl I once was. I was completely enchanted with the prospect. Without hesitation, I called Jane and asked her what she thought my next move should be. She said that Amabella, her agent friend, would probably want to meet with me in person, and that perhaps I'd need to be prepared to get myself to New York City. *New York City!* The *Big Apple!* The little I knew about New York I'd witnessed through Sarah Jessica Parker and her posse from the HBO series *Sex and the City*. Just like my vision of attending San Francisco State, it was a dream coming true. Although I didn't like to fly, if it meant the difference between getting an agent or not, I'd find a way to manage the journey.

Amabella's email instructed me to email or call. I called and we arranged to meet the following week, as she would be coming to San Francisco. I marveled at my luck.

Prada, nada.

Things began to happen quickly. I got a few other replies from agents in New York, including one who represented authors ranging from adult popular fiction to African American young-adult novelists. She told me my story should be situated in a beauty shop, given that was how *we*—meaning black folks—usually congregated. I didn't think my story was *that* book. We bid each other adieu and I nursed the cold sores that broke out on my mouth as a result of having to tell her no. I prepared to meet Amabella, whom I had a good feeling about. I suggested to her that we meet at the Campton Place Hotel, which was only a few blocks both from her hotel and my salon, and I appreciated the Campton's dependable service and elegant quietude. After my partner and I opened our salon in the Shreve Building, her mother had not only stood in as our receptionist, but had also treated us to dinner at the Campton for five nights straight.

"Hey there!" Amabella called out as she made her way to our table. "Sorry I'm a little late."

"Not even," I said, appreciative of her meeting with me and wanting to make things nice. She wore dark-rimmed glasses, black Sven clogs—the kind nurses and Lainey wore—black capri slacks, and a multicolored blouse. I was a little surprised—from the fashion magazines, I'd thought the New York look was more like trench coats, folded-hem jeans, and black Prada kitten heels. Clearly, Amabella wasn't one to be influenced by New York Fashion Week.

"I'm so glad we could meet this way," she started off. "The timing is great—I'm also in town to scout out a place to open our agency's West Coast office."

"Get outta here!" I said.

"Serendipitous, right?" Amabella said. "Anyway, let's talk about you, and this amazing story you've written."

Had I heard her correctly? Had she said my story was *amazing*?

I'd also read someplace that I needed to imagine what I wanted for myself regarding my book. I'd grabbed the pink section of the *San Francisco Chronicle* and flipped to the *New York Times* bestseller list. I cut that section out and brushed a line of Wite-Out through the number-one book slot and printed in the name of my book over it. I asked Amabella if she thought, like J.K. Rowling, I might get a two-book contract, and maybe even a million-dollar advance. Amabella then advised me of what her last client received for her memoir, and it was nowhere near a million, let alone a two-book deal. But something in me said, *believing is seeing.* I wrote down that I was going to get a two-book deal. I liked Amabella, and I decided that she was the best agent to represent me.

At her suggestion, I arranged to travel to New York City. Before I left, I wrote down something else: the six-figure numbers I believed my story was worth.

I was in a superstar film

"This reminds me of *The Bluest Eye*," an editor from Little, Brown said. Amabella and I sat across from her. Hers was an imprint of one of the seven largest publishing houses in the world, Time Warner Book Group. I'd heard of *The Bluest Eye*, had a copy of it, and I'd browsed through a few of its pages before putting it down because I freaked out that someone could capture the voice, tone, and cadence of black experience so poignantly, my own experience in many ways. Truth be told, I hadn't felt smart enough to appreciate what the complexity of the narrative was trying to say.

Two days prior, I'd arrived by train at Penn Station and taken a taxi to SoHo. I was to stay in Amabella's family flat near the Hudson River. Arriving in New York had been like something out of a fairy tale. After debarking from the train, I was met by a redcap who grabbed my suitcase and escorted me to a set of escalators. I felt like I was in a film with the way I ascended from beneath that dazzling city and stepped onto Seventh Avenue. I was my very own Funny Girl.

Each of those few days I awoke in New York City brought with it another meeting with this person and that one. From the moment I awoke till the time I dropped, fully clothed, onto the bed at the end of a totally packed day, it was all about who wanted the book as it was, who wanted me to change the title, and (lastly) who wanted me to make it about Miss Kerr being a lesbian, so that I might ride the tailwinds of E. Lynn Harris's work. I stuck to my story as it was. Though I remained open to changing the title if needed.

The ancestors

On my last day in New York, I decided to ditch Amabella's agenda in favor of my own. I left the flat before she called to tell me all the different places she'd expect me to meet her. Also, I was exhausted from telling the story of Jeanne and me. Each time seemed to hammer in the fact that even though I wrote about her, I had to deal with the sadness of not having her around. I found myself suddenly wishing for her to be there with me in that city, watching me run through stores like the wild and crazy child that was alive and well inside me.

For hours, I walked through SoHo. When I worked at Vidal Sassoon, all the stylists talked about SoHo and the freedom and individuality that were expressed through the hair and fashion giving the place its name and reputation. From Canal Street to Broadway, on over to Broome, Spring, and Prince streets, I perused the shops. I stopped in at Kate's Paperie and grabbed a box of thank-you cards. I planned to fill them out on the train and mail them to all the editors, as well as to Amabella, her team, and her mother.

Given I didn't own a cell phone at that time—believing that I would burn brain cells at twice the normal rate if I did—I found a public pay phone to call Joanne, Amabella's mother. I wanted to check in to see if my son or anyone from my salon had called. "Where the heck are you?" Joanne asked, her voice pitched with high energy. I told her I'd been shopping, having some fun, having a Julia Roberts *Pretty Woman* time. She told me that Amabella had been calling every few minutes looking for me, and that I needed to give her a ring.

"OMG . . ." Amabella said when she picked up the phone, "Where are you right now?" Like I had with her mother, I recounted what I was up to.

"You did it," she said. I was unsure of what she meant.

"I did what?" I asked.

"*Everyone* we met with wants to acquire your manuscript." Amabella said. *Everyone.* I was quickly swept up into that old familiar feeling of being scarecited.

"The editor at Warner has made an offer." Amabella told me the dollar amount and I had to do everything I could not to scream my face off.

"What does this mean?" I asked.

"It means we can either take the offer, or we can ask for what you want and see what happens. Or we can ask for an auction. What do *you* want?" Amabella asked. It took only a moment for me to know which way I wanted to go. In some way, I felt that I wanted to honor my African ancestors. I didn't know who they were, but I also knew I hadn't come that far on my own. In that moment, I felt compelled to attribute a portion of my success to them. Also: I imagined black bodies on auction blocks, with no choice and no voice, sold to the highest bidder. In a much larger way, I imagined that my writing had come to me by way of my ancestors. I felt I could not in good conscience let my story be sold in that manner. *I* had a choice. I remembered walking into my soon-to-be editor's office at Warner Books. She was so soft-spoken, inviting, and kind. I told her my story and I saw the tears well up in her eyes. I appreciated that she saw me. It helped me feel as though I wasn't a freak, and although I may not have had the nuclear family model growing up, I had a story worth telling.

"I'd like to go with Warner," I told Amabella.

"Okay!" Amabella said. I loved her calm demeanor. "And you accept the offer on the table?"

"Nope. Let's start with asking for a two-book deal," I told Amabella.

"You got it. I'll keep you posted!"

We had to move quickly. I told Amabella that if for some reason

Warner changed their minds, I had a second and third choice. She instructed me to go and buy myself a cell phone.

A burner phone in my one hand—should Amabella need to contact me as I traveled across the country via Amtrak—and the treats from my SoHo trip in another, I boarded the Lake Shore Limited, which would take me from Penn Station to Chicago, where I'd catch the California Zephyr to get home. I was anxious to get back into my little sleeper compartment, think back over those last few days, and smile myself all the way across our great big nation. I beamed, imagining Cinderella herself would've been envious of me.

Four days later, I stood in my salon, staring out of the window at the San Francisco end of the Bay Bridge. On a clear day, we had a clean view of the bay through the maze of buildings that made up a good portion of Union Square. Earlier, I'd received the phone call from Amabella. The editor at Warner had agreed to the two-book deal. When Amabella asked how much I wanted, I told her the number I'd written down before I'd left for New York.

"Thank you for calling Keter Salon, how may I help you?" I always answered the phone the same way.

"Re . . . gi . . . na . . ." I recognized Amabella's voice. I was terrified she'd called to tell me that the big New York editor wanted me to know where I could shove my ridiculous request.

"It's a deal. She gave you what you asked for."

"Thank you, Amabella . . . for everything," I said.

Proof

My manuscript delivery date had been set: we were to release my book in
June 2003. From the moment my editor, Elyse, sent me the email letting
me know her expectations, I spent every waking moment rewriting and re-
reading the contents of my book. At the same time, I continued my search
for Jeanne Kerr, and the more I wrote about her, the more questions the
adult part of me had regarding the child in me that she left behind. It was
difficult to imagine that Jeanne had turned her back and forgotten about
me. To keep moving through the plot, to keep shaping our story, I'd have
to keep convincing the adult part of me that the Jeanne my younger self
had known would've never disappeared of her own accord.

The more I processed Jeanne in the writing and rewriting, the more
sightings I had of her. I saw her in the shoulder of a woman who rounded
a corner. It was the way her shoulder dipped to avoid bumping into anyone. I'd walk up to the woman and before I had a chance to speak, the
truth revealed itself. I saw her in the movement of a dark-haired woman
who sashayed down the street, the same way Jeanne had, her steps quick-
like. Certain. Sometimes I saw her pushing a baby carriage; other times
her arm was entwined in her lover's as they ambled down the street, love-
sprung all over one another.

Once, upon the recommendation of a client, I enrolled in a weekend
self-improvement workshop. It offered attendees "a permanent shift in
the quality of your life." On day two, Jeanne showed up—she was blond
then, her hair layered and shoulder-length. While everyone else hurried
through the doors to get into the room and find their seats, she glided in.

Her entrance and the way her clothes flowed like gossamer immediately captured me.

The workshop divvied us up by twos; the "ones" formed one single-file line through the room and the "twos" stood opposite them. I was a one. The facilitator gave specific instructions. We were to grab the hands of the people on our immediate right and left for balance, and then, when we were ready, stare unwaveringly into the face of the person standing directly across from us. The idea was for each participant to create and hold a space of loving kindness by looking deeply into *your* person's eyes without breaking contact.

As fate would have it, I stood opposite of this Jeanne.

She was remarkable, Jeanne was. She gazed into my eyes, and although she didn't exactly smile, the corners of her mouth softened, lifting her eyes ever so slightly into the most compassion-filled expression I'd ever seen. I felt the love and kindness she graciously extended to me. I, however, wasn't so capable. I soon became overwhelmed by the fact that I couldn't shake my projections. I got caught in a cycle of rolling my eyes and sighing heavily, to the point of breaking down in tears.

This Jeanne continued holding the space. The more exact she was, the more difficult the task became for me. Before long, it was as though the woman who'd once hand made me a blue corduroy dress, with a rainbow of colors that arched across the breastbone, was there in front of me. I'd worn that dress until I lost it somewhere between moving into foster home number eight and Guideways. For a moment, it seemed as if I were *actually* standing across from the Jeanne of my childhood years. Completely freaked out, I struggled to prevent everyone from seeing me lose my composure.

There I was, a thirtysomething woman who'd obviously hallucinated in front of a hundred strangers. I nearly fainted from the public embarrassment. At lunch, I was given an option to leave early, which I felt compelled to accept.

Safe in my apartment, I filled the bathtub to the rim. With a cooking thermometer, I tested the water until it reached ninety-eight degrees—the same temperature as the human womb. I put on Pachelbel's "Canon in D" and stepped into the tub. For a moment, I sat there and listened to the sorrowful mourn of the violin chords, letting them soften me. Then, ever so slowly, I dipped beneath the surface. I imagined that I was inside my mother, tethered to her in spirit, and then I balled my hands into fists and mouthed the scream I'd been holding for far too long. "How do I let you go?" I chanted until I exhausted myself. I allowed the warmth and the depth of her womb to absorb my rage, my shame, and my pain. I was my own mother.

Through everything, I continued to rework my book. It was all going well—that is, until I received a sucker punch from Elyse.

"I need you to find someone to corroborate your story," Elyse asked. We were just a few months away from going to press. I'd turned in the manuscript on time—doing my part, or so I thought. The word *corroborate* landed hard between us. Incriminating. I felt as if I were being accused of lying, or worse.

"What do you mean?" I asked.

"We need you to find someone to verify what you've asserted in your memoir," she explained.

Only two weeks to find *that* someone? I felt somewhat optimistic—until Elyse also requested an author photo to place on the cover of my book.

I sat at my desk and stared at the photos that stairstepped across the walls in my writing studio, most of them of my son. There was also the painting my partner had given to me on my fortieth birthday. A portrait of a little black girl. Blue dress. Peter Pan collar. Amber eyes. She looked as close as I remembered to what I might've looked like as a young girl, freckles, pigtails, and all. But the portrait had no say in the matter, the portrait didn't have the power to say that what I declared had happened had indeed *happened*, say that the life I lived was real, mine, and that I didn't make it all up.

While Elyse's deadline loomed, I decided to try to locate my father. Even though I remembered all too well how he hadn't recognized me, I told myself he'd be better than having no one. I took BART to San Francisco. I got off the train at the same spot I'd seen him before. He was not there. He was not there each of the five days I returned and waited for him.

At this point in my career, I was booked with clients four months in advance. I chopped, styled, and sewed in hair for everyone from Rebecca Walker to Sandra Bernhard. I'd even assisted in the hand dyeing of an ultra-red-magenta snap-on ponytail for Lady Miss Kier from the band Deee-Lite. In between all the highlights, perms, color touch-ups, and blow-dries, I scoured the internet looking for Jeanne. Into search box after search box, I typed in what I knew about her. Marriage license? Nothing. Birth certificate for a child? Nothing. Death certificate? Hesitantly, I punched in her name into that search box, bracing myself for news of *my* Jeanne's death. Eventually that too came back with: nothing. Maybe I had made Jeanne up; maybe she was proof of my unreliable memory. But, what about the blue corduroy dress she'd hand sewn, rainbow arching across the breastbone? The way she called me "Sweetheart," or "Punkin'"? The way she smelled of Cream of Wheat with warmed PET Milk, vanilla, and brown sugar?

Return to sender

Contra Costa County Department of Human Services boomed from the sender's envelope. *Return to Sender if Undeliverable* was emboldened beneath the county's address. I was relieved to be home the day it arrived. I nestled the large manila package in the crook of my elbow. It was a newborn.

I opened the envelope and removed its contents. A half-inch stack of pleading papers filled to the margins with legal jargon took up most of the envelope's contents. These were like the incident reports I'd read after breaking into those file cabinets. Unlike the original file, this envelope held half of the contents I'd remembered reading. There were the incident reports of the various violations I'd committed. There were the letters from one institutional director to another justifying my need to be "terminated." I looked for the psychiatric diagnosis of my being "manic-depressive turned bipolar," and having "oppositional disorder" and "failure to attach."

I searched for the incidents regarding my time spent in the security-housing unit (the SHU box) at Guideways Residential Treatment Center. Boot to chest, back to floor, my face turned to the concrete. Orderlies holding me down. There were none of the medical consent forms Gwen Forde had sworn that my father signed, saying it was fine to treat me with psychotropic drugs. The woman I'd spoken to at the county office had warned me of their vetting process. "We won't give you everything that's in the file." My expectations were low.

But out from between the pages glided an envelope, alighting on the floor. It was small. I'd never seen it before. Once white—I imagined—it had been patinaed by age to a rusty sort of gold. It was one of several letters Jeanne had written:

May 17, 1977

Dear ███████ and Dr. ████████████,

I am sending a copy of this to both of you.

I would like it to be known that I would like to be a foster parent, with the hope of one day adopting Regina, if it is in any way in her best interest.

I have heard that it's very unlikely that foster home placements be granted to employees—so am aware of this.

The natural feeling of caring and loving is there. I will do anything possible to help her mature.

I feel Regina needs lots of attention and firmness as well as someone she can trust and communicate with. I feel that I meet these needs. She needs to know her limits explicitly and have them followed through. The need for lots of attention has been very evident during her stay at ECS. I'm sure you are aware of all the "incident reports."

I will gladly take Regina to therapy appointments and I also will be happy to participate in therapy with Regina if so desired.

I realize that Regina is an active and talented person in many ways and will require dedication and commitment to encourage the development of her potential. I love her and I think I fully realize the commitment I will be making.

Hopefully Regina will discuss with both of you the fact that her father told her this weekend that he's going to L.A. One of his songs made the ratings and another that he sings is being promoted. Regina said last time he went to L.A. like this he was gone for a year or more. Regina said that he was planning on sending for his wife and their children when he got settled. Regina says she doesn't wish to live with him anyway, but is hurt he is leaving.

I am looking for another job and hope to find one soon—this would also eliminate potential difficulties in being considered for foster parenting.

A move will also be required if there is a possibility of Regina being placed with me, as my apartment does not allow children. I have located several apartments, which do take children, for a change of residence.

I also do not know of any group home in Contra Costa Co. that does not have heavy drug traffic as well as being permissive sexually.

Regina has limited experiences in these areas and I feel it's unadvisable to expose her further to these elements. Regina is very impressionable and guidance and example are extremely important.

There are strong ties between Regina and her father, as well as between Regina and her grandmother and Regina and her mother. Hopefully Regina can someday feel better about her relationship with them.

I also realize one of the goals may be to reunite Regina with her kin. I will do all I can possible to help Regina mature. The commitment is here within me. I will look forward to hearing your professional opinion—what do you feel is best for Regina?

I am doing all that I can to get the foster care license. Regina needs to get into school, as well as get settled into her new home soon. Her wait to be placed has been almost half a year.

I would also like to be at Regina's institutional staffing on Tuesday to offer my input, or just sit in on the process. Will await your word on this, ████.

Regina does not know of my desire to be her foster parent. She does not know that I will be sending a note along to both of you when she leaves for her appointment tomorrow.

Most Sincerely,

Jeanne Kathleen Kerr

Resume included to hopefully give additional information on my background. I want to help Regina in any way possible, every way possible. Again thank you, Jeanne.

Russian Red

With only a few days left to corroborate my story, or else change all the names of the characters in the book, and with no leads from the county's file, I became desperate. I asked Julia Scheeres, a friend and fellow author, to help me find Jeanne. A correspondent at *Wired* magazine, she had access to databases unavailable to people like me. I gave her Jeanne's full name, her birth date, and approximate age.

The return from LexisNexis brought a list of names and addresses that matched the information I'd given her regarding Jeanne. The results showed Jeanne living but a few miles from where I lived, in Walnut Creek. That's where she'd lived when we were younger. I printed out the addresses and drove to the first one on the list. I shook with expectation. Grief. Confusion. Rage that we'd possibly lived so close to one another without either of us being aware of it. Rage that had she, or anyone else, bothered to just look in the Whitepages under my name, they would've found me. I had always made sure to make it easy for anyone who wanted to find me.

I searched from the Avila Garden Apartments, located off Boulevard Way, to the Flora Apartment Homes, on Flora Drive. I remembered that place; it was where I'd gone when I'd run from the shelter decades before. Unbelievable. How she could have lived in the same place for so long was amazing to me. Since my time in care, I'd moved as many times as I had while in care.

"Yes?" a woman's voice answered at a condominium complex. There was no name on the front of the building, only an address.

"Does Jeanne Kerr live here?"

"What is your name?" the voice replied. Something in the way she asked made me feel hopeful. I'd not heard Jeanne's voice in so long; I imagined it had changed with age.

"My name is Regina. I—"

"She hasn't lived here in more than twelve years," the voice said.

"Do you know where I might find her?"

"No, I don't, sorry."

I made my way home. When I looked at the sheet Julia had given me, I realized that in my excitement I'd read the addresses incorrectly. Jeanne hadn't lived in the area for more than fifteen years. There was another address, of an army base in Fort Campbell, Kentucky. I tried calling the associated phone numbers.

"Hello?" The voice at the other end was hushed, similar to Jeanne's. ". . . Is anyone there?"

"Yes. May I speak with Jeanne Kerr?" I crossed my fingers.

"Yes, who is this?" the voice cracked.

"It's Regina Louise, I think we may've met a—"

"I don't believe so," the stranger interrupted, her voice turning a shade defensive.

"Did you—"

The line went dead.

"—ever work at the Edgar Children's Shelter?"

That latest Jeanne, and the other three I called, joined the long list of crossed-off Jeannes whose numbers I'd scribbled on a well-thumbed notepad. I wrote a letter to the last address on the list Jules had given me. I purchased fine linen paper with rounded edges. In two lines, I asked *that* Jeanne if she remembered me. I sealed the envelope with a kiss in Russian Red lipstick.

Addressee unknown

The deadline passed. As a result, at the publisher's urging, I changed all the names of all the characters and settings in my manuscript; I ended up giving Jeanne the name Claire. For the cover of the book, Elyse approved a stock photo of a young brown-skinned girl holding an umbrella, her identity obscured. The cover was beautiful, but my sense of erasure felt bone-deep.

Warner was supporting my book with a tour slated for ten cities: Berkeley, Portland, Seattle, Vancouver, Oakland, San Francisco, Los Angeles, Claremont, and Pasadena, ending in New York. Along the way I gave interviews and everyone asked about "the woman in the book who once loved you."

"Do you know her whereabouts?" some asked. "Has she ever reached out for you?" others inquired. My answer was always *no*.

In between the questions, I thought about the letter that sat at the bottom of my purse. Bright red letters spelled out *Addressee Unknown*. Ever since it had been returned to me, a week after I mailed it, I carried it in my purse, a secret reminder that I was tired of looking for people who clearly weren't looking for me.

In Los Angeles, I was interviewed by Tavis Smiley. It was the first time on the tour I hadn't felt bombarded with questions about Jeanne. He focused more on my biological family, and asked my opinion about Ruby's inability to parent me. I was generous, I felt. I explained that I did not know for certain, but my best guess was that she didn't have what she needed to succeed as a person first, then as a mother. I mentioned something to the effect that Ruby didn't have her faculties about her, and that life for her had been hard.

"You have it all," Tavis had said. "A thriving business, a well-adjusted son, a new book. What more could you ask for?"

"I want someone to tell me that they are proud of me," I said. "I want someone who knew me when I was that foster girl no one wanted, I want someone to bear witness to what I've done with my life."

After the interview, back at the Mondrian on Sunset Boulevard, I headed straight to my room, kicked off my shoes, and sat for a moment. Certain that I'd received the next day's itinerary from Kim-from-LA (my publicist), I scrolled through my emails and came across one with a subject line that read: *I am so proud of you, sweetheart!*

Had someone from Tavis's office transcribed my interview and sent it to me? I opened the message.

It was from Jeanne.

Evidently an old coworker named Holly Eckwall, someone who had worked with Jeanne during the time we were both at the shelter, had read a newspaper article about me and reached out to her.

She had a son, Jeanne did. He was twenty-six years old. She was on her way to California to bring him back to Alabama, where she and his father, her husband, were living. "Please reach out to me once your tour is done. I don't want to be a bother."

Speechless. Stunned. Knocked to six. How could I be certain it *was her?*

What will I call her?

"Hello?" The voice at the other end of the line had a hushed timbre. Her way of saying *hello* softened me from the inside out.

"You were my first child," she told me. Her words reverberated: *my first child.* My ears were caverns. Even now, writing these words more than a decade later, the commotion that moment stirred feels indescribable.

"I have something I want to give you. It is your birthright," Jeanne said. *Me? I have a birthright? She has something to give me?* I was overrun with emotions. It had been a lifetime since we had seen one another.

"I want to make you my daughter," Jeanne said. *Her daughter?* There I was, twenty-seven years of no birthdays between us, no holidays, no rites of passage celebrated, and no photos that stairstepped up or down the walls of her den.

We were both quiet.

What will I call her?

New York City, 2003

What should I wear to meet the woman who once wanted to be my mother?
It was 9:00 p.m. eastern time. I was standing in the middle of my room
at the Paramount Hotel in New York City, staring trancelike into the
mirror. I was unable to calm my nerves long enough to decide on which
shoes to wear: the leopard peep-toe heels or a pair of Cynthia Rowley
wedges from last season. I kicked both across the room and peeled the
wet blouse away from my skin. The sweaty silk, similar to the paper-thin
membrane that clings to the inside of an eggshell, was limp. The room,
hardly bigger than a walk-in closet, was hot and sticky, which made
moving around a job unto itself.

New York City was the last stop on my tour. Apart from the early-
morning interviews and afternoon book signings at the Harlem Book
Fair and the Schomburg Center for Research in Black Culture followed
by a CNN panel featuring Wendy Williams, Pamela Newkirk, and a few
other authors I'd never heard of, I'd spent what was left of the day flying through the best shops Manhattan had to offer. After speaking with
Jeanne on the phone that morning, I'd realized I had nothing to offer her.
I needed to show my appreciation for her agreeing to meet me. I wanted
to wipe the chalkboard clean of the Regina she thought she knew. I wasn't
asking for anything; I'd learned how to fend for myself. She had admitted
to having a chocolate addiction. I power walked twenty-four city blocks
to get to the nearest Godiva store. I arrived just as the store was closing. I slipped a $100 bill into the crack between the two front doors and
pleaded with the store manager to let me in.

Having scored at Godiva, I added that treat to the pile that included a blue pashmina scarf, which the saleslady had placed so carefully into the signature Henri Bendel box with brown and white stripes, and a golfing shirt I'd purchased for Jeanne's husband from Bergdorf Goodman.

It wasn't just that I loved shopping, or giving folks nice gifts—which of course I did. It was about me not wanting Jeanne to have the wrong impression. It was important that she didn't think of me as that emotionally disturbed girl, so severely disturbed that she wasn't allowed to adopt me. That was why, I imagined, she hadn't wanted anything to do with me. I wouldn't say as much when we met up. I didn't plan to accuse her of anything, but I was aware that those thoughts were welling up in me.

By the time Jeanne's plane was finally scheduled to land, at 11:30 p.m., it had already been delayed three times. There had been a tropical storm near the Florida city where Jeanne had boarded her plane. At 10:00 I ran through the lobby of the Paramount and climbed into the back seat of a Town Car. I loved that in New York, I could get a hired car for almost the same price as a taxi. Over the wet streets we cruised, past the Lunt-Fontanne Theatre, where earlier *Beauty and the Beast* had lines around the block, through Times Square, where life popped off all around us. It was hardly believable: I was *finally* on my way to meet Jeanne.

I want to make you my daughter swirled around my mind the entire ride to the airport. I wondered what that meant, how being a daughter felt, and how and when I'd know the difference. Upon arrival at LaGuardia, I asked the driver, Pierre, a Dominican gentleman, to wait for me. I wasn't clear how long Jeanne's plane would take to land, but still, I was willing to incur any additional cost to ensure she wouldn't have to wait in the rain for a taxi after flying through a storm.

The waiting area was small. Most of the people there looked as though they had been sitting for far too long. I took a seat that provided a clear view of the information monitor. Every few minutes or so, I'd stand and get a close-up of the screen, scanning for more updates. A few times I stood only to smooth any wrinkles from my skirt. I'd spent the last part of the afternoon trying to decide on flat shoes versus high heels, black versus pink. I'd brought three full-sized suitcases on the journey, one entirely empty for the shoes I was certain to buy in SoHo. I had lots to choose from.

I had imagined for years what it would be like to see the woman who wanted to be my mother. How would I want her to see me? Dress after dress, pants, shirts, and even a ball gown later, I'd picked a chocolate-colored, mid-length skirt, a long-sleeved T-shirt, and a pair of soft-pink Mary Jane wedges. I wanted to look approachable—not too serious, not too New York–like. I wanted Jeanne to feel comfortable. And I wanted the girl in me, who had waited so long for this, to feel good. Safe. Beautiful.

By 11:45, I'd been waiting more than an hour, and my thoughts moved from how exciting it was going to be to see Jeanne again to images of Jeanne dying in a plane crash. Visions of an aircraft plummeting, then twirling through the open sky, not only crossed my mind again and again, but it was as though I felt the rush of turbulence in my own body. My anxiety twisting, I had to scold myself: *Don't think those thoughts.* The scolding morphed into acceptance: *If that's the case, and she crashes, I'll be okay—just knowing I've found her, that she remembered me enough to say she'd never stopped loving me. That was far more than I ever expected.* I forced myself to lean into faith.

A little after midnight, Jeanne's flight landed.

"Hi, sweetheart!" She called from the plane. "We just landed." I'd given up relying on the information screens. I was beyond wanting her to arrive.

"I'm waiting in the receiving area. Need any help with your bags?" Jeanne's phone cut out before she could answer. I moved closer to the opening that led from the jetway. My mind began to somersault. I felt like a fraud. *What am I doing? Who do I think I am? Really, Regina?!*

I white-knuckled my handbag, straightened my back, and clamped my heels together. I held on to myself like never before. I didn't want to appear too excited. I didn't want to be too much. People began to disembark. A man, a woman, another man, two women. A woman wearing a black baseball cap with *Mercedes-Benz* stitched in red block letters above the bill moved toward me. *That's not her.* Another woman wore a sweater with colorful daffodils and peonies on it that swallowed the top half of her body. *No, that's definitely not her.* The woman acted as if she recognized me. *Tell me those are not lime-green capri pants with white polka dots; tell me those are not kitty-cat socks.*

"Sweetheart?!" the gray-haired stranger with the wildlife-inspired attire screamed. Loudly. And for a brief moment I was flushed with teenaged mortification. It was official: I was a daughter.

Jeanne placed her hands upon my face, leaned her forehead onto mine, and held me. I remained speechless. When I finally said something, it was to ask her to follow me. Once outside, and when we were safely in the back seat of the car, Jeanne handed me a small photo album. I didn't dare look at it. I placed it in my handbag.

We sat in silence all the way back to the hotel. I can't speak for her, but the tears streaming down her face said it all. As for me, the only word that fit the occasion, the only phrase bold enough, cool enough, funny and wild enough to hold the magnitude of the moment was *verklempt*, a word I'd learned long ago from my friend Robyn at San Francisco State. I was absolutely and unequivocally verklempt.

I'd reserved a room for Jeanne on the eighth floor of the same hotel I'd been staying in. We opened her door and there, on the table, were the gifts I'd purchased earlier. We sat, and I offered her the boxes one after the other. The blue pashmina looked great with her skin tone. I hoped she could see that I could pay my own way, that I would not be a burden.

"You shouldn't have, sweetheart," is what Jeanne said as we sat, her on the chair next to the table and me on her bed.

"It's the very least I can do," I said.

"Look at you," Jeanne said through the strain of holding back tears, "you're . . . all grown-up."

I didn't know what to say, and even if I had, I wouldn't have known how to express the indescribable. She, too, had grown up. Her ponytail was more than two feet long, streaked with gray. I was envious of the life she'd lived to earn that gray. Her skin, quite pale, was tighter to her face, and her smile rested deeper into her chin.

The best I could do was sit. I'd worked hard at learning to do just that. Sit. Wait. Watch what showed up. Pick my battles. Cultivate generosity. Compassion. When Jeanne stepped into the bathroom, I pulled the photo album from my handbag. My heart jackhammered as I ran my fingers along the brown leather cover. I was afraid of what I'd find. So, for a moment I just sat there, tried to relax. Eventually, I peeled the cover back, and there I found a handwritten inscription:

Dearest Regina
Here are a few photos capturing the birth of our lifetime heart connection.
With all my love,
Momma

I turned to the next page, and there in front of me was the cutest young girl. Her vibrant brown skin glistened, and she smiled while hugging a stuffed animal. She appeared content. She looked kind. As for me, I didn't remember if I loved that stuffed animal or not. I didn't remember if I'd asked for him, or whether I had received him as a "gift," the way so many foster children did, from a box of donations for Christmas or Easter or some other random reason that I no longer remembered. Although I'd wanted to, I didn't know that girl, her hair, her style, the way she hugged—no—clutched the stuffed tiger, the way her eyes looked out, inviting me in. I couldn't make the leap from where I was—in a Philippe Starck hotel in New York's Theater District, wearing an expensive hair-weave, on a book tour—to the place *that* girl was asking me to remember. I'd grown accustomed to the book-cover me, the unidentifiable girl in the tattered yellow dress who belonged to no one. As much as I wanted to belong, I was deathly afraid that I wouldn't know how to, that I might somehow mess it up. I wasn't ready to look *that* girl in the eye, to locate her in space and time, to acknowledge in full how I'd had to leave her behind for the adult me to be where I was, then. She was the one no one wanted. I'd need time to catch up to her, to get to know and remember her. I closed the album.

Epilogue

When you grow up the way Regina Louise grew up—abandoned by her parents, physically abused by caretakers, shuttled from foster home to foster home—you learn to doubt your memories. Even the good ones, especially the good ones, come with a disclaimer: Maybe they never happened....

In 1975, on the eve of her 13th birthday, Louise arrived at a children's shelter in the Bay Area city of Martinez. Jeanne Taylor worked at the shelter, and where others saw bad behavior in Louise, Taylor saw potential....

Taylor wanted to adopt the girl....

But some social workers ... preferred to place black children with black families, believing those homes to be more suitable settings. Taylor was white, single and 31.

The court denied her petition to adopt.

That denial meant Louise would spend the rest of her childhood moving: She lived in at least 30 homes and facilities....

Even as life got better, the past continued to dog Louise. She decided that writing a book was the best way to let go.

—*Los Angeles Times*, 2005

Jeannie ended up marrying a military man, having a son and moving to the South. Regina was never adopted and left foster care at age 18. When she attended San Francisco State on scholarship, she had no name to offer when asked for an emergency contact. She had no place to go when the dorms closed for school breaks. There was not a single person in the world who claimed her as family....

But soon after her first book, "Somebody's Someone," was published last summer, Jeannie—whose last name is now Taylor—heard about it and sent an e-mail through Regina's Web site.

—*SFGate*, 2004

Ms. LOUISE: All I really wanted was to find someone, be it Jeanne Kerr, be it anyone who could have known me, many, many years ago, and who could have said to me, "I'm proud of you," based on the fact that I had written a memoir and I'm okay, I'm breathing, I'm successful. I went upstairs, I turned on my computer because I needed to do some work, and there's an email with the banner "I am so proud of you, sweetheart." I couldn't take it in, I'd lost my footing and the air that I would normally breathe in so easily became challenging. And I just tried to sit with that. I decided I'm going to call her, and I called her. And I was like, "Hi. May . . . I . . . speak . . . with Jeanne Kerr?" She's like, "(Gasping) Sweetheart, is that you?" And I didn't know how to respond and I just sat there.

She's like, "Sweetheart, is that you?" She said, "You know, I never stopped loving you. You were my first child, and I never stopped loving you." I just listened and I just said, you know, "You're my mommy." She's like, "Yes, I know. You are my baby."

Ms. TAYLOR: When she called and said she had been looking for me and I thought, "My goodness, I wasn't lost," you know what I mean? "I was there all the time. How could she not find me?" I mean, it was an anomaly to me, you know? Here I was not trying to hide, and if she'd been looking for me, I was surprised.

Ms. LOUISE: And we reunited in New York in July.

—*All Things Considered*, 2003

When they met again, the first thing Taylor did was hand Louise some photos of herself at age 11. "Until then, I had never had a photo," Louise said.

"I took lots of pictures and always had two made, one for her and one for me," Taylor said Saturday. "She couldn't keep hers, but I did."

In 2003, 25 years after that Contra Costa judge denied the adoption, Jeanne Taylor adopted her long-lost foster kid, who became Regina Louise Kerr-Taylor.

It happened in the same Martinez courtroom where they were turned down a quarter century earlier.

—*East Bay Times*, 2005

Dearest Regina ♡

Here are a few photos
capturing the birth of
our
lifetime heart connection.
With all my love,

Momma

Regina Louise holding a donated tiger
April 1978

Elizabeth Kerr (Jeanne's mother), John Kerr (Jeanne's son), and Regina Louise
December 1978

Regina Louise with her father, Tom

June 1978

Judith Kerr (Jeanne's sister) and Regina Louise

back row, left to right: Doug Taylor, Michael Adelakun (Regina's son), Judge Lois Haight, Christopher Taylor; front row, left to right: Regina Louise Kerr, Talia Kerr, and Jeanne Kerr
November 20, 2003

A talisman given to Regina by Jeanne on the day of their adoption.

Acknowledgments

To my eleven-year-old self, on bended knee I say to you: thank you for knowing the difference between being loved and unloved, and taking the risk to go out into the world to find what was best for you, and ultimately us. I love you, Gina-girl.

To the children lost in foster care adrift: may you be found, remembered; may you know your claim, allow yourself to be claimed; and may you always know your name.

To my family of friends, and those who I am forever bonded to in whatever ways that means to you: thank you. I see you, and I love you.

To my professors at California Institute of Integral Studies: there is such freedom in learning what is mine and what isn't. Thank you, for teaching me to know the difference.

To my professors at UCR (you know who you are): I am indebted to your generosity of time.

To my therapists, who to this day are still willing to help me keep putting Humpty back together, again.

Last, but not least: thank you Susan Straight for taking me under your wing.

Questions and topics for discussion

This is a book club discussion guide for *Someone Has Led This Child to Believe* by Regina Louise. It includes suggested discussion questions, which may help spark new and interesting conversations in your book club.

1. Regina often creates an alternate reality to fill a void in her life. ("My philosophy was to use my imagination to see things the way I thought they should be, and maybe one day could be, and work to no end to make things happen," page 154.) In this way, how does Regina use her imagination to create hope for herself in a dark situation? Discuss some examples of Regina using her imagination to escape from her circumstances.

2. Jeanne Kerr gave Regina a dictionary and instructed her to "never skip over a word you don't know" (page 85). Throughout her life, how does Regina's understanding of words and their meanings empower her?

3. Create a list of Regina's strengths and weaknesses. How do they change at different points in her life?

4. On page 103, how does the use of repetition—"Man, y'all gotta take me off this mess"—affect her message? What did she convey to you in that passage?

5. The story is broken up into four parts. Why was it presented this way, and what role does each part play in Regina's journey?

6. How did reading confidential documents about Regina make you feel? Do you think Regina's life course would have been different if she hadn't seen them? How?

7. Regina reads the contents of her personal file as a teenager. How might her reaction to that information have differed at other stages in her life—at age 20? 30? 40?

8. The book's title is taken from a letter on page 132: "Between you and me, I think someone has led this child to believe she is above-average intelligence when she is marginal at best." How did you interpret the title before experiencing it in its full context? After reading that paragraph, did your interpretation change? How?

9. Regina later believes she will "never make it to the center because I was destined to be trapped within the small and ill-defined borders of the margins" (page 135). How is she able to overcome this and eventually "make it to the center," as she puts it?

10. Jeanne Kerr stays in Regina's mind long after they've been separated. How does Jeanne help alter Regina's perception of herself, even when she's not physically there? How does Gwen Forde?

11. Regina has a fraught relationship with Gwen Forde. What motivates Regina when she is with Gwen? And vice versa?

12. At graduation (page 144), Regina and her choir mates perform "I Sing the Body Electric" from the musical *Fame*. Listen to the song and pay close attention to the lyrics—how do they mirror Regina's own feelings at that moment in her life? Why do you think she chose this particular song?

13. Pick a passage that stood out to you. What elements made it memorable?

14. Regina fixates on the idea of belonging—to trauma, to a person, to a system, etc. For Regina, what does it mean to belong to something? What does she belong to at the beginning of the story? At the end?

15. Regina, somehow, learns the value of keeping "silent vows." How was she able to do so, and why do you imagine it was important for her to do so?

16. Trauma-informed care is a relatively new approach to working with children who have experienced trauma. It emphasizes that when understanding trauma, it is more effective to ask "what happened?" to a person, rather than asking "what's wrong?" with a person. How might Regina's experience in foster care have been different if she had received trauma-informed care?

17. Did you have any preconceived notions about the effects of childhood trauma before reading the book? If so, did the role trauma played in Regina's journey affect those notions? Why or why not?

Q&A with author Regina Louise

Someone Has Led This Child to Believe is, in many ways, a follow-up
to your first memoir, *Somebody's Someone*, published in 2003. What
compelled you to write this book at this time in your life?
This book interrogates trauma and the aftermath of broken souls left in
its wake. I believe I better understand—more so now than when I was
writing my first book—how to navigate the varying degrees of trauma,
loss, and abandonment, as well as the intersectionality, that come with
growing up in (and aging out of) out-of-home care and foster care. These
situations often cause incredibly challenging human emotions and dilem-
mas. For twenty-plus years, I've been healing my traumas and rewiring
behavior patterns from my past. I've learned to change habituated ways
of responding to experiences and traumas. I am an adult now, and I have
a better sense of my own agency, protective factors, and inner strengths,
all of which aid me in reaching back into the dark and facing powerful
and emotionally charged memories.

Since writing your first book, you adapted it into a play, and also
earned an MFA in creative writing at University of California, River-
side. How has your work as a writer evolved since you wrote *Somebody's Someone?*
With my first book, I didn't know what I didn't know. Writing that
book was a purely organic reaction to a disorienting experience I had.
I could have behaved badly—very badly—toward myself, which is how
I learned to survive and stay safe as a child (by never holding an adult

accountable for his/her behaviors). Instead, I ran home after the challenging event and picked up a pencil instead of a razor blade (or worse). Then I found a piece of paper, instead of a handle of vodka. I sat down and listened to the small voice inside me, rather than the bullying, dark side of my nature that tried to convince me I wasn't worth the effort it would take to listen to my gut.

This book, my second, is shaped and/or inspired by various authors I've read and respect. That's what grad school did for me: it gave me studio time to begin the process of learning who and what I was in relation to the craft of writing. I learned the importance of research and the importance of spatial and temporal realities and how those realities affect people whose lives are carved by trauma. So this book is different in that way.

Your book deals with so many painful experiences. Were there any parts that were particularly challenging to revisit?
Writing about my womb-mother was particularly challenging, mainly because I'm certain the chance for us to get to know one another and perhaps engage in courageous and radical conversations is gone. Thank the Lord I got me some education and deep personal healing because it has helped me elevate my perspective from victim to victor.

I now better understand the historical conditions that aided and abetted not only my mother's failure but also the generational underachievement and lack of opportunities that are synonymous with being born black. As I state in my book, I am grateful for the journey: it has given me the privilege to transform my devastation into my motivation.

What do you hope readers will take away from Someone Has Led This Child to Believe?
The indestructible nature of the human spirit, and the importance of keeping one's solemn vow—especially to one's self.

You were adopted after the publication of *Somebody's Someone*. What was that experience like?

Great question! Unfortunately, there's nothing close to enough white space to answer this question here. Stay on the lookout for book three!

What's next for you?

Book three. More coaching. Maybe a PhD. Maybe a television show where I am coaching people into their highest and greatest version of themselves. Maybe a professorship. I'm open.